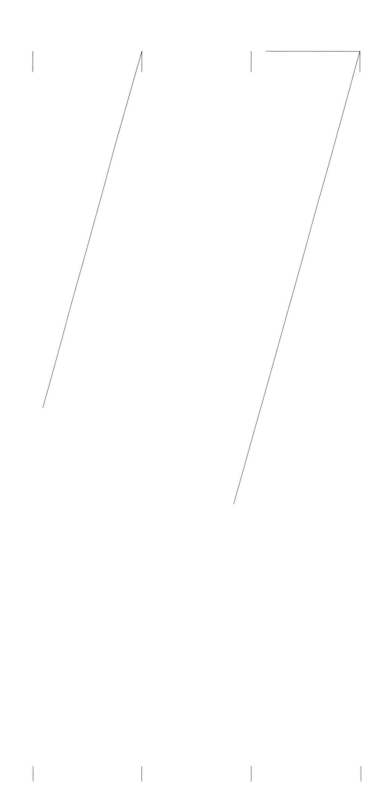

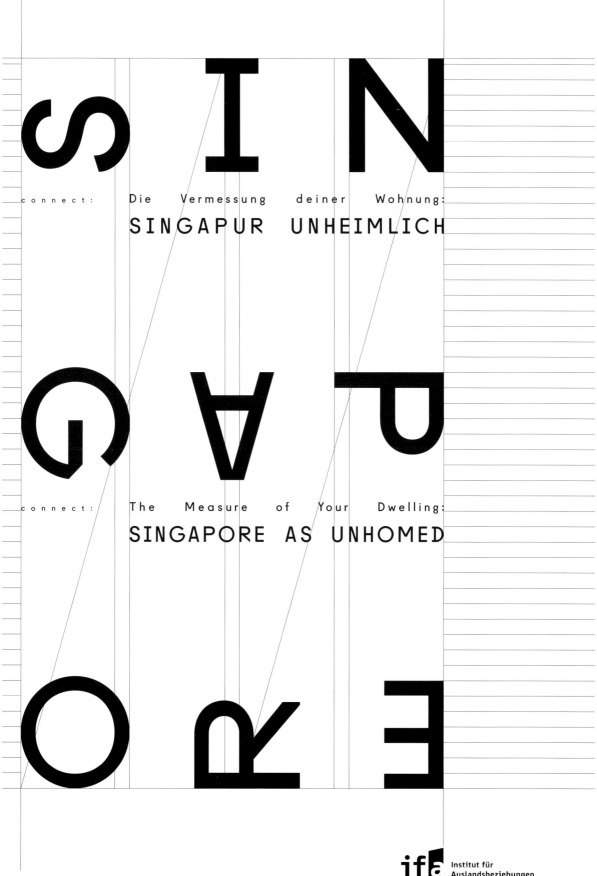

INHALT / CONTENT

VORWORT 13
PREFACE 17

DIE REINHEIT DER EINHEIT ZERRÜTTEN 22
CHARLES MEREWETHER

UNSETTLING THE PURITY OF ONE 28
CHARLES MEREWETHER

DAS MASS DES WOHNENS: 35
SINGAPUR UNHEIMLICH
JASON WEE

THE MEASURE OF YOUR DWELLING: 41
SINGAPORE AS UNHOMED
JASON WEE

KÜNSTLER / ARTISTS

ASHLEY YEO 48
IM GESPRÄCH MIT / IN CONVERSATION WITH GREGORY COATES

CHARLES LIM 58
ÜBER MEIN VIDEO / ABOUT MY VIDEO

CHUA CHYE TECK 62
IM GESPRÄCH MIT / IN CONVERSATION WITH TRICIA LIM

CHUN KAI FENG 72
ÜBER MEINE ARBEIT / ABOUT MY WORK

GERALDINE KANG 76
IM GESPRÄCH MIT / IN CONVERSATION WITH SYLVIA POH

GRACE TAN & RANDY CHAN 86
IM GESPRÄCH MITEINANDER / IN CONVERSATION WITH EACH OTHER

HO TZU NYEN 92
IM GESPRÄCH MIT / IN CONVERSATION WITH JASON WEE

JEREMY SHARMA 100
IM GESPRÄCH MIT / IN CONVERSATION WITH JOHN CHIA

TAN PIN PIN 110
DREI FRAGEN / THREE QUESTIONS

VINCE ONG 114
IM GESPRÄCH MIT / IN CONVERSATION WITH KELVIN ANG

ZAI TANG 120
IM GESPRÄCH MIT / IN CONVERSATION WITH JOLEEN LOH

ESSAYS / ESSAYS

WIEDER NEU MACHEN 131
MICHAEL LEE

MAKING NEW, AGAIN 135
MICHAEL LEE

DAS SINGAPORE ART ARCHIVE PROJECT: 140
VON YISHUN IN DIE GILLMAN BARRACKS
KOH NGUANG HOW

THE SINGAPORE ART ARCHIVE PROJECT: 148
FROM YISHUN TO GILLMAN BARRACKS
KOH NGUANG HOW

SINGAPUR ALS GARTENSTADT: 162
DIE TECHNO-ORGANISCHE HEIMAT
MAY EE WONG

SINGAPORE AS GARDEN CITY: 168
THE TECHNO-ORGANIC HOME
MAY EE WONG

WIR SIND ALLE *FREMDE* 174
ANCA RUJOIU

WE ARE ALL *FOREIGNERS* 177
ANCA RUJOIU

BIOGRAFIEN / CVS 184
IMPRESSUM / IMPRINT 192

V O R W O R T

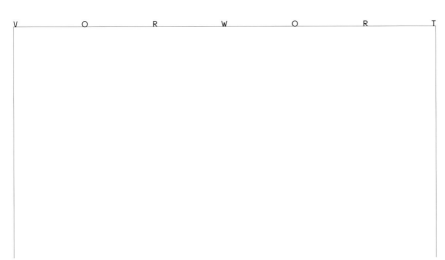

Die ifa-Galerien Berlin und Stuttgart zeigen die Ausstellung *Die Vermessung deiner Wohnung: Singapur unheimlich* als sechstes Projekt innerhalb der Ausstellungsreihe *connect*. Begonnen wurde die Reihe 2009 mit *Kunstszene Vietnam*, einer Ausstellung, in der wie 2012 in *Rosige Zukunft – Aktuelle Kunst aus Tunesien* und 2013 in *Phnom Penh: Das Verschwinden verhindern. Zeitgenössische Kunst und Stadtentwicklung in Kambodscha* die aktuelle Kunstszene eines Landes vorgestellt wurde. Mit *A Gentil Carioca: Ein Kunstraum in Rio de Janeiro* sowie *Khoj: International Artists' Association Delhi* boten die ifa-Galerien zwei international agierenden und renommierten Kunsträumen die Möglichkeit, ihre Arbeit in Deutschland vorzustellen. Die Ausstellung *BY NOW – Zeitgenössische Fotografie aus Belarus* bot in dieser Reihe einen Ein- und Überblick über die aktuelle Fotografie-Szene in Belarus.

connect: Verbinden, kontaktieren, vermitteln, zusammenbringen, zuschalten wird das Institut für Auslandsbeziehungen e.V. in den ifa-Galerien Berlin und Stuttgart in einer losen Folge von Ausstellungen, Veranstaltungen und Publikationen verschiedene Szenen im Bereich der bildenden Kunst in Afrika, Asien, Lateinamerika und Osteuropa. Der in *connect*: enthaltene Imperativ richtet sich nicht nur an die Institution, sondern auch an die Besucher; er erinnert an die Aufforderung „Only connect!" des englischen Schriftstellers E. M. Forster, der Anfang des 20. Jahrhunderts mehrere Jahre in Indien verbrachte und 1924 in *A Passage to India* ein kritisches Porträt des britischen Kolonialismus in Indien zeichnete und die damit zusammenhängenden Konflikte zwischen Ost und West thematisierte. „Only connect!" fordert dazu auf, auf den anderen zuzugehen, Beziehungen zu knüpfen und über diese nachzudenken, Ideen, kulturelle Unterschiede und Ähnlichkeiten wahrzunehmen und zu diskutieren – „Sei offen!", wie dies auch das Motto des Instituts für Auslandsbeziehungen propagiert: *Kulturen verbinden, connecting cultures*.

In der globalisierten internationalen Kunstwelt werden grundlegende Fragen noch immer nur punktuell und allzu oft einseitig, von einem westlichen Standpunkt aus diskutiert; und auch wenn scheinbar überall alles bekannt ist, so sind es doch immer einzelne, wechselnde Städte, Regionen oder Länder, die im Fokus der internationalen Aufmerksamkeit in der Kunstwelt und des Kunstmarktes stehen; derzeit ist wieder

VORWORT

einmal ein China-Hype zu verzeichnen. Es gibt aber immer Szenen, nationale, regionale oder lokale Kunstszenen, auf welche derzeit nicht das Hauptaugenmerk der internationalen Kunstwelt gerichtet ist, in denen sich jedoch spannende Entwicklungen vollziehen – sei es, dass durch die Initiative einzelner oder einer Gruppe von Kreativen neue Räume für Kunst entstehen; sei es, dass durch politische, wirtschaftliche und gesellschaftliche Veränderungen auch neue Entwicklungen im Kunstbereich möglich wurden.

Die ifa-Galerien laden ein, bieten eine Plattform zur Vorstellung, zur Begegnung, zur Auseinandersetzung und zum Diskurs; sie bieten die Möglichkeit, Beziehungen zu knüpfen, Netzwerke aufzubauen und zu erweitern mit zurzeit äußerst aktiven Kunstszenen, mit einzelnen Kunstinstitutionen auch außerhalb der derzeit im Fokus stehenden Zentren, mit Künstlerinnen und Künstlern, Küntslergruppen, Kuratorinnen und Kuratoren. Wir laden unsere Kooperationspartner und unsere Besucher dazu ein, über das Verhältnis von Globalem und Lokalem in der Kunst nachzudenken, über Begriffe wie Tradition und universeller Moderne zu diskutieren, unterschiedliche Rahmenbedingungen künstlerischer Produktion und die Funktion von Institutionen zu erkunden, Kriterien und Maßstäbe zu hinterfragen – im Austausch, im Dialog mit Künstlern, Kuratoren, Publizisten und anderen Protagonisten im kreativen Bereich aus Hanoi oder Delhi, Rio de Janeiro oder Minsk: only connect!

Singapur ist als Insel- und Stadtstaat ein besonderer und spannender Ort. Die zeitgenössische Kunstszene wird deutlich dadurch charakterisiert, dass Singapur Schmelztiegel unterschiedlichster künstlerischer Richtungen und kultureller Prägungen ist. Künstlerinnen und Künstler[1] aus ganz Asien und der Welt nutzen mehr und mehr den regional optimal gelegenen Standort, um dort zu leben und zu arbeiten, um Teil der Kunstszene mit Ausstellungen, Konferenzen, Symposien und Festivals zu sein. Nicht zu vergessen die Singapore Biennale, die alle zwei Jahre ein großes die Stadt beherrschendes, internationales Kunstereignis mit zahllosen Events und Ausstellungen rund um das Singapur Art Museum ist.

Andererseits erfordert die begrenzte Fläche der Stadt eine sehr flexible Stadtplanung und –entwicklung. Der permanente Rückbau älterer Bausubstanz bringt es mit sich, dass kaum ein Areal von der ständigen Erneuerung verschont bleibt. Neue Technologien rufen sofort neue Bauprojekte auf den Plan, die immer gigantischer werden und die Stadt in zunehmenden Maße beherrschen. Dies betrifft nicht allein die Skyline Singapurs sondern vor allem die Organisation des Lebens der Bewohner, die die Bereiche ‚Arbeiten, Leben, Erholung' von der Architektur zugewiesen bekommen, ohne individuelle Ausweichmöglichkeiten zu haben, weil die nötige Fläche fehlt. Die Künstler setzen sich mit diesem Phänomen in unterschiedlichster Art und Weise auseinander. Sie manifestieren in ihrer künstlerischen Arbeit, dass dieser stete Wandel Einfluss auf die Mentalität der Bevölkerung und natürlich auch auf Kultur und Kunst hat. Der Zwang, sich immer wieder neu orientieren zu müssen, wird von den Einen als aufregend und inspirierend empfunden, von den Anderen dagegen als irritierend, weil es so etwas wie Heimat nicht mehr gibt und Erinnerungsorte für immer verschwinden.

VORWORT

Mit diesem Projekt beteiligt sich die ifa-Galerie Berlin an den Asien-Pazifik-Wochen Berlin (2015), die zum wiederholten Male in Berlin stattfindet und unter dem Motto *Smart Cities* stehen. „Die APW Berlin 2015 richten den Fokus auf Smart Cities und thematisieren die urbanen Herausforderungen, die sich in Berlin und den Wachstumsmetropolen Asiens stellen. Experten präsentieren Modelle zur intelligenten, digitalen Vernetzung und optimalen Steuerung von Städten sowie zukunftsfähigen urbanen Technologien aus den Bereichen Energie, Mobilität, Ressourcen- und Umweltmanagement, Kreislaufwirtschaft sowie digitale Infrastruktur. Im Fokus des Dialogs mit den asiatischen Partnern stehen die Interdependenzen von Smart Cities, Green Economy und nachhaltiger Entwicklung." (aus dem Flyer der APW 2015) Die Ausstellung thematisiert dieses und stellt Künstlerinnen und Künstler vor, die sich mit diesen spezifischen Problemen in ihrer künstlerischen Arbeit auseinandersetzen. Kurator ist Jason Wee aus Singapur, der nicht nur als Künstler, sondern vor allem Kurator zeitgenössischer Kunst und in der Kunstszene Singapurs zuhause ist.

Wir danken den Künstlerinnen und Künstlern, den Autorinnen und Autoren für die gute Zusammenarbeit. Unser Dank gilt Frau Siew Lan Moh, Goethe Institut Singapur, die das Projekt mit großem Interesse verfolgte und Jason Wee, dem Kurator der Ausstellung. Unser Dank geht ebenso herzlich an Jennifer Teo, Urich Lau Wai Yuen, Amanda Heng, Koh Nguang How und Ute Meta Bauer, die mir wertvolle Informationen und Hinweise zur Kunstszene Singapurs gegeben haben.

Dem Auswärtigen Amt der Bundesrepublik Deutschland, das unsere Arbeit im Rahmen Auswärtiger Kultur- und Bildungspolitik trägt, gilt unserer besonderer Dank.

Barbara Barsch
Februar 2015

---

[1] Im Folgenden wird aus Gründen der Texteffizienz und des Leseflusses generell das generische Maskulinum genutzt. Selbstverständlich sind damit immer beide Geschlechter gemeint. Im Einzelfall, etwa bei Überschriften, kann hiervon abgewichen werden.

PREFACE

The ifa Galleries Berlin and Stuttgart present the exhibition *The Measure of Your Dwelling: Singapore as Unhomed*, the sixth project in the series *connect:*. The series began in 2009 with *Art Scene Vietnam*, an exhibition that introduced the current art scene of one country, and was followed in 2012 by *Rosy Future—Contemporary Art from Tunisia* and in 2013 by *Phnom Penh: Rescue Archaeology. Contemporary Art and Urban Change in Cambodia*. Two internationally active and renowned art spaces were given the opportunity to present their work in the ifa Galleries in Germany with *A Gentil Carioca—An Art Space in Rio de Janeiro* and *Khoj International Artists' Association, Delhi*. The exhibition *BY NOW. Contemporary Photography from Belarus* offered an insight and an overview of the current photography scene in Belarus.

connect: join, contact, introduce, bring together, link up. In a loose series of exhibitions, publications and events in the ifa Galleries in Berlin and Stuttgart, the Institut für Auslandsbeziehungen will connect various scenes in the field of visual arts in Africa, Asia, Latin America and Eastern Europe. The imperative contained in connect: is directed not only to the institution, but also to the visitors. It recalls the challenge to "Only connect" issued by the English writer E. M. Forster, who in the early 20th century spent a number of years in India and in 1924, in *A Passage to India*, drew a critical portrait of British colonialism in India, addressing the resulting conflicts between East and West. "Only connect" encourages us to reach out to others, to build relationships and to reflect upon them, to recognize and discuss ideas, cultural differences and similarities—to "Be open!", as indicated in the slogan of the Institute für Auslandsbeziehungen: *Kulturen verbinden, connecting cultures*.

In the globalized international art world, fundamental questions are still discussed only occasionally and all too often from a one-sided, western point of view; and even though it seems that everything is known everywhere, still there are ever-changing individual cities, regions or countries, that become the focus of international attention in the art world and the art market; currently a China hype is once again evident. But there are always scenes, national, regional or local art scenes, which are not at

PREFACE

the moment the main focus of the international art world, in which however, exciting developments are taking place—whether it is the appearance of creative new spaces for art through individual or group initiatives; or whether it is new developments in the field of art made possible by political, economic and social changes.

The ifa Galleries provide an invitation and a platform for presentations, encounters, debates and discourse; they offer an opportunity to build relationships, to establish and expand networks with art scenes that are currently very active, with individual art institutions which are outside the centres currently in focus, and with artists, artist groups and curators. We invite our partners and our visitors to reflect upon the relationship between the global and the local in art, to discuss concepts such as tradition and universal modernity, to explore various contexts of artistic production and the role of institutions, to question criteria and standards—in an exchange, a dialogue with artists, curators, writers and other protagonists in creative fields in Hanoi or Delhi, Rio de Janeiro or Minsk: only connect!

Singapore as island—and city-state is a special and exciting place. The contemporary art scene is clearly characterized by the fact that Singapore is a melting pot of highly diverse artistic tendencies and cultural influences. With its optimal location in the region, it is more and more being used by artists from all over Asia and the world as a place to live and work, to be part of the art scene with its exhibitions, conferences, symposia and festivals. Not to mention the Singapore Biennale, a major international art event which every two years dominates the city with countless events and exhibitions centred around the Singapore Art Museum.

On the other hand, the limited space of the city requires very flexible urban planning and development. The permanent restoration of older buildings has the effect that almost no area is spared from the constant renewal. New technologies immediately lead to plans for new construction projects which are ever more gigantic and increasingly dominate the city. This affects not only the Singapore skyline but also the organization of the lives of residents, whose "working, living, recreation" areas are dictated by architecture without having individual alternatives, because the necessary space is lacking. Artists address this phenomenon in widely differing ways. They manifest in their work that this constant change influences the mentality of the population and of course culture and art as well. The necessity to constantly reorient oneself is seen by some as exciting and inspiring, but by others as irritating, because there is no longer such a thing as home and locations that hold memories disappear forever.

With this project, the ifa Gallery Berlin participates in the Asia-Pacific Weeks Berlin (2015), which takes place once again in Berlin, this year with the theme *Smart Cities*. "The APW Berlin 2015 will focus on smart cities and in particular the urban challenges facing Berlin and the high-growth cities of Asia. Experts will be presenting models for intelligent digital networking and city management optimization as well as urban technologies of the future from the fields of energy, mobility, resource and environmental management, recycling management and digital infrastructure. The main focal point of the dialog with our Asian partners is the interdependence

PREFACE

between smart cities, the green economy and sustainable development." (From the flyer of the APW 2015) The exhibition addresses this and introduces artists who deal with these specific problems in their artistic work. Curator is Jason Wee from Singapore, who is not only an artist, but also a curator of contemporary art and is at home in the Singapore art scene.

We thank the artists and the authors for their cooperation. Our thanks to Ms. Siew Lan Moh, Goethe Institut Singapore, who has supported the project with great interest and Jason Wee, the curator of the exhibition. Our thanks also goes to Jennifer Teo, Urich Lau Wai Yuen, Amanda Heng, Koh Nguang How and Ute Meta Bauer, who gave me valuable information and tips on the art scene in Singapore.

Our special thanks goes to the German Federal Foreign Office, which supports our work in the context of foreign cultural and educational policy.

Barbara Barsch
February 2015

DIE REINHEIT DER EINHEIT ZERRÜTTEN

CHARLES MEREWETHER

Der Titel dieses Projekts kann als rhetorischer Ausdruck verstanden werden, der die folgende Frage stellt: Was ist das Maß des Wohnens? Er steckt die Idee des eigenen Wohnraums ab, der Heimat, des Landes, und auch der Nation. Und doch ist dies kein Ausgangspunkt – das fiktive Narrativ der Anfänge –, ein Fixpunkt der Bestimmung oder der Referenz, sondern vielmehr ein Raum der Verortung. Das Projekt bezieht sich dabei auf den Kulturtheoretiker Homi Bhabha, der seine Konzeption des „Unheimlichen" beschreibt als „eine Erfahrung, in der das Gefühl des sicheren, persönlichen Wohnens ebenso wie die allgemeine öffentliche Welt irritiert wird, sodass sowohl das Private wie das Öffentliche immer fremder und unübersichtlicher werden." Damit hat Bhabha das Bezugsfeld von Freuds Begriff des „Unheimlichen",[1] der sich auf das Individuum und dessen persönliche Erfahrung der Entfremdung von Vertrautem bezieht, erweitert. Diese Entfremdung erzeugt Angst, überschreitet gewohnte Grenzen zwischen dem Vertrauten und dem Unvertrauten, Grenzen zwischen Innerlichkeit und Äußerlichkeit oder dem Privaten und dem Öffentlichen. Mit seiner Konzeption bezog Bhabha sich allerdings auch auf Derrida und dessen Lesart von Freuds Begriff des Unheimlichen als auf Angst begründet.[2] Diese Angst lässt uns mit uns selbst unbehaglich fühlen, auf eine Weise, die eine drohende Auflösung unserer Subjektivität zur Folge hat.

Bhabha versteht das „Unheimliche" in einem umfassenderen sozialen Bezugsrahmen, indem er von der Erfahrung des Kolonialismus und von Formen des Widerstands der Kolonisierten ausgeht und sich auch auf die Schriften und die Kulturkritik

---

1   Vgl. Sigmund Freud, *Das Unheimliche* (1919), in: Ders., *Studienausgabe, Bd. IV: Psychologische Schriften*, Frankfurt/M. 1982: Fischer, S. 241–274.

2   Jacques Derrida, *Dem Archiv verschrieben. Eine Freudsche Impression*, Berlin: Brinkmann und Bose, 1997.

Edward Saids bezieht, insbesondere auf dessen Buch *Orientalismus* (1978). Hiervon ausgehend schreibt Bhabha, als Einwurf gegen die in den 1980er Jahren vielfach verkündete Vorstellung des Multikulturalismus, das Szenario um und erlaubt so eine Untersuchung der kulturübergreifenden Beziehungen zwischen Menschen und Ethnien. Bewaffnet mit Begriffen der Ambivalenz, der Hybridisierung und der Mimikry, richtet Bhabha sein Augenmerk auf die kulturelle Differenz im Unterschied zur kulturellen Diversität. Denn während kulturelle Diversität Gegenstand des empirischen Wissens ist, wird kulturelle Differenz diskursiv durch einen Prozess der Artikulation konstruiert. Dieser Prozess ist ein Mittelweg zwischen Entdecken und Erkennen. Dieser Intervention durch Bhabha folgte eine enorme Flut von Texten, in denen die Kulturgeschichte von Zivilisationen seit der Eroberung Amerikas vor über fünfhundert Jahren umgeschrieben wurde. Und während die Anwesenheit und die Anerkennung von Hybridität eine Errungenschaft ist, hat sich an ihrer Vereinnahmung unter dem Signum der kulturellen Diversität und dem Prozess der Selektivität und der Assimilierung oder der Exklusion dennoch nichts geändert.

Doch wie leitet dies nun zum Fall Singapur über, ein Land, das nicht älter als fünfzig Jahre ist, dessen komplexe Geschichte der Entstehung als Nation allerdings eng mit seinen Nachbarn Malaysia, Indonesien, Indien und China verstrickt ist? Zudem ist der Kontext für dieses Projekt das zeitgenössische Kunstschaffen in Singapur. Hier ist weniger der Begriff der Hybridität von Bedeutung als vielmehr der des Unheimlichen.

Es ist bemerkenswert, wie schwer die Erfahrung Singapurs auf dem Bewusstsein vieler singapurischer Künstlerinnen und Künstler lastet. Sie verspüren ein Unbehagen darüber, einer Nation anzugehören, so als wäre die Identität, Singapurer zu sein, tiefgreifend unbefriedigend bis hin zur Verunsicherung. Das soll nicht heißen, dass dies nichts bedeute, es bedeutet zu viel! Es ist belastend. Doch worum handelt es sich? Vielleicht können wir mit der Erklärung beginnen, dass es das Gewicht eines Staates ist, der als Nationalstaat anerkannt werden will, als eine souveräne Macht, als eine Kultur, die weder ein Fortsatz Chinas ist noch einfach bloß ein weiteres südostasiatisches Land. Insbesondere über diese letztere Kennzeichnung versucht Singapur hinauszugelangen, wenn es diese Länder zu repräsentieren beansprucht, wie es etwa in den Ambitionen der Nationalgalerie zum Ausdruck kommt, die 2015 eröffnen wird. Die Verkürzung dieser komplexen Geschichte auf die Geschichte Singapurs wirkte sich auch auf die ethnische Gruppe der Peranakan aus, deren zeitgenössische wie vergangene Geschichte auf die Flure der historischen Vergangenheit und der Museen verbannt wurde. Darüber hinaus versucht der Staat, durch seine Finanzierungs- und Förderungsstrategien die zeitgenössische Kunstszene zu reglementieren. So bietet der National Arts Council Stipendien und Ateliers für jene Künstler, die als würdig erachtet werden, in den letzten Jahren insbesondere für jene, die den Begriff der ‚Gemeinschaft' hochhalten. Die Gemeinschaftskunst wird gefeiert, was auch immer dieser Begriff bedeuten mag, solange er nur genannt wird.

Fundamental für die Erfahrung des Unheimlichen ist die Weise, wie das Vertraute fremd gemacht wurde, eine Erfahrung, die eine verstörende Wirkung auf die Häuslichkeit selbst hatte. Wie Jason Wee bemerkt: „… die Ambivalenz, die einerseits von einem Charakter erfahren wird, der mit den ‚allgemeinen Antagonismen der politischen Existenz' verbunden ist, und die andererseits ein Gefühl für den Ort ist, das sich, durch Zögern, Mangel oder Entfernung, selbst verbirgt oder gar auslöscht. Diese Ausstellung und mein Essay bieten mir die Gelegenheit, den Schwerpunkt vom Literarischen hin zu den räumlichen Dimensionen des Unheimlichen zu verschieben – zu dessen Infrastruktur, der Stadtplanung, der gebauten Vertikalität, der Organisation unserer Bewegungen, des Erbes, des Orts."[3]

An einem Ort, wo die Heimat und die Häuslichkeit im alltäglichen Leben so zentral sind, dringt diese Verstörung auch in die globalere Sphäre von Fragen der Identität, der kulturellen Entwurzelung und des Exils ein. Hinzu kommen die Auswirkungen der Informationstechnologien auf den einst gesicherten Mythos der häuslichen Privatsphäre und der Familie als virtueller Gemeinschaft. Das technologische Netzwerk erweitert die Grenzen der Häuslichkeit, während die Mobilität in ihr Zentrum eindringt und den Begriff der Privatisierung selbst verändert.

In diesen Diskussionen ist latent auch eine Neudefinition der Gemeinschaft enthalten, nämlich das Verständnis einer Gemeinschaft, die weder singulär ist noch beschränkt auf die Heimat oder die Nation und all das, was diese Faktoren nach sich ziehen. Denn wir sprechen hier über das Gefühl der Zugehörigkeit, das der Begriff der Gemeinschaft impliziert. Darüber hinaus wird dieses gemeinschaftliche Leben als Einheit repräsentiert, als Zusammenhalt einer Identität, die für die Singularität der Nationalität steht, wie etwa Singapurs. Dies ist die moralische Kraft der Gemeinschaft als Einheit, es ist nicht die Ethik der Singularität. Vielmehr ist es die Forderung nach Repräsentation (und nach Reproduktion), die die Vorstellung der Gemeinschaft als plural, widersprüchlich, als Differenz ausschließt. Darüber hinaus ist die Nation, wie Benedict Anderson in seinem Buch *Die Erfindung der Nation* so stichhaltig argumentiert hat,[4] ein symbolischer Raum, dessen ideologische Reinheit als Reaktion auf die Angst vor ihrer Kontaminierung konstruiert wird. Diese Gefahr der Kontaminierung ist die Erfahrung des Unheimlichen oder das, was die vorgestellte Sicherheit der „Heimlichkeit" der Gemeinschaft und die Souveränität der Nation zu sprengen droht.

In diesem erdrückenden Kontext versuchen Künstler in Singapur heute, die Atmosphäre anderer Kulturen zu atmen. Einige ziehen es vor, nicht singapurisch genannt zu werden, andere fliehen einfach, absolvieren eine Künstlerresidenz, die wiederum dazu dienen kann, den Aufenthalt an einem anderen Ort auszuweiten, während wieder andere einfach von Station zu Station reisen, sei es mithilfe von Ausstellungen, Stipendien oder der Gastfreundschaft Dritter. Ist das, was aus dieser Rastlosigkeit von in Singapur lebenden Künstlern entstanden ist, eine Untersuchung bestimmter Antagonismen? Um dies zu beantworten, möchte ich auf den Moment der „Artikulation" der kulturellen Differenz zurückkehren. Denn dieser Moment eröffnet ein viel beweglicheres Umfeld mit der Möglichkeit der Veränderung, ein Widerstand gegen oder eine Abkehr von jeder Typisierung oder Fixierung oder der Projektion einer Reinheit, die als homogenisierende Kraft dient, um die Gemeinschaft unter

---

3   Jason Wee, Notes for Curatorial Proposal, unveröffentlicht. Wir werden an Anthony Vidlers Argumentation erinnert, dass dem „Unheimlichen" eine architektonische Dimension innewohne. Vgl. Anthony Vidler, *The Architectural Uncanny*, Cambridge, Mass., MIT Press, 1994.

4   Benedict Anderson, *Die Erfindung der Nation. Zur Karriere eines folgenreichen Konzepts*, erw. Neuausg., Frankfurt/M.: Campus, 1996.

dem Signum einer nationalen Identität zu vereinigen. Folgt man dieser Argumentationslinie, dann ist die Kultur nichts Vorgegebenes. Dann besteht keine Gewissheit in der Idee eines traditionellen oder festen Bezugspunkts wie der Heimat oder des Staates.

Zwei der für diese Ausstellung ausgewählten Künstler und eine Künstlerin arbeiten vorrangig mit Film oder Video: Tan Pin Pin, Charles Lim und Ho Tzu Nyen. Die vielfältigen Kunstpraktiken dieser Künstler unterscheiden sich deutlich voneinander, können jedoch auf einen Nenner gebracht werden, als Kritik an der Essentialisierung des Staates als souveräne Nation durch die „Reinigung" ihrer Geschichte und ihres Ursprungs und durch die ideologische Konstruktion einer „Gemeinschaft".

Im Jahr 2001 präsentierte Tan Pin Pin *Moving House*. Dieser Kurzfilm befasste sich mit der Umsiedlung Tausender Familien, die gezwungen worden waren, aus ihren dörflichen Gemeinschaften in moderne öffentlich geförderte Wohnungsbauten umzuziehen. In vielerlei Hinsicht korrespondiert diese staatliche Politik mit der Zwangslage chinesischer Familien, die vom chinesischen Staat aus ihren traditionellen Hutongs in Wohnhochhäuser umgesetzt wurden. Diese Gemeinschaften wurden dadurch zerstört, und an ihrer Stelle wurde die typische Atomisierung des modernen städtischen Lebens, wie sie im Westen üblich ist, geschaffen. Die Filmemacherin integrierte in ihrem Film darüber hinaus die Erzählung einer dieser Familien, die gezwungen worden war, die sterblichen Überreste ihrer Angehörigen von einem Friedhof in eine Urnenhalle umzubetten. Darin wurde eine unausgesprochene Parallele evident.

Später hat Tan den Film *To Singapore, With Love* (2013) über die schwierige Situation von sechs politischen Exilanten geschaffen, die alle „verschiedene ideologische Positionen vertreten und unterschiedlich alt sind; einige sind Kommunisten, andere Aktivisten aus der christlichen Linken, wieder andere sozialistische Politiker oder ehemalige Studentenführer."[5] Der Film wurde von der Regierung Singapurs jedoch sofort verboten, weil er „die nationale Sicherheit unterminiert."[6] Vielleicht hat die Regierung Recht, vielleicht aber auch nicht. Ihre pauschale Zensur scheint kontraproduktiv. In einer Demokratie würde eine öffentliche Vorführung unterschiedliche Meinungen und Bewertungen erlauben, die auf den veröffentlichten Zeugnissen basieren, und die Menschen könnten sich ihre eigenen Gedanken machen. (s. S. 110)

Im Jahr 2011 produzierte der Künstler Charles Lim das 20-minütige Video *All the Lines Flow Out*, das einer mysteriösen Figur auf ihrem Weg entlang den longkangs – die örtliche Bezeichnung für Abwasserkanäle – folgt, die sich als gewaltiges Netzwerk über den gesamten Stadtstaat Singapur ziehen.[7] Man könnte meinen,

---

5   Statement von Tan, *Notes from Serangoon Road*, 2014.

6   Der singapurische Minister für Kommunikation und Information, Dr. Yaacob, meinte, dass der Film „*To Singapore, With Love* Unwahrheiten und Täuschungen über diese Geschichte enthält". Und weiter: „Die öffentliche Vorführung eines Films zu erlauben, der den bewaffneten Aufstand einer illegalen Organisation sowie gewaltsame und subversive, gegen die Bürger Singapurs gerichtete Aktionen verschleiert und beschönigt, würde letztlich bedeuten, die Anwendung von Gewalt und Subversion in Singapur gutzuheißen und würde insofern unsere nationalen Sicherheit gefährden."

7   Die folgende Passage zu Charles Lim verwendet Material aus einem meiner Essays: *Future Imaginaries*, in: *Asian Connectivities*, hg. v. Michelle Antoinette und Caroline Turner, Canberra: Australian National University, 2014.

die Figur sei auf der Suche nach einem Weg nach Hause. An die rätselhaften Landschaften Andrei Tarkowskis erinnernd, schafft Lim die mysteriöse endzeitliche Welt eines Baudelaire'schen Flaneurs. Und doch unterlagen diese longkangs mit der Zeit allmählich den Diktaten von Singapurs beinahe zwanghafter Besessenheit, sich als moderne Stadtlandschaft selbst zu konstruieren. Diese Konstruktion missachtet die schrankenlose Kraft der Natur, die offensichtlich wird, wenn die Stadt durch den Monsun lahmgelegt wird, der Springfluten mit sich bringt, die bis in das Zentrum des Einkaufsviertels reichen können.

Lim hat seinen Blick auf Singapur auch auf die Topografie des Landes ausgeweitet, um festzustellen, dass selbst diese gegenüber der Regierungslogik des Instrumentalismus und ihren Zielen nicht immun ist. In einer Reihe von Kurzfilmen und Installationen unter dem Titel *Sea State* untersucht Lim das konkrete Wachstum der Stadt Singapur durch das Aufhäufen von Sand an ihren Ufern – Projekte der Land-„Gewinnung", wie sie genannt werden –, wofür Sand von kleineren Inseln ausgehoben wurde, die zu Indonesien und anderen Nachbarstaaten gehören.[8] Dadurch stand Singapur an der Spitze der Liste von Ländern, die tatsächlich materiell gewachsen sind. Diese Vorhaben wurden schließlich eingestellt. Doch wie David Teh über das Projekt *Sea State* bemerkt, hält es fest, wie die „maritime Geografie fast gänzlich aus der nationalen Bildwelt und der Alltagserfahrung ausgelöscht" und durch auf dem Festland basierende Stadtvisionen ersetzt wurde.[9] (s. S. 58)

Ho Tzu Nyen sagte über einen seiner frühen Filme, *Utama: Every Name in History is I* (2003), er sei „ein Versuch, das Gespenst von Utama heraufzubeschwören". In einem Artikel, der in der Zeitschrift Forum on Contemporary Art and Society (2007) veröffentlicht wurde, zeichnet Ho die Geschichte nach, wie „Katzen – große und kleine, wilde und domestizierte, eingebildete und reale – auf enigmatische Weise mit der Geschichte Singapurs verwoben sind." Durch die Kombination mythischer Legenden und historischer Fakten über die Gründung Singapurs wendet sich Ho Fragen zu, die mit der Konstruktion von Identität oder Identitätspolitik in Bezug auf den Staat und die Nationengründung verbunden sind. Letztlich handelt dieser Film von der „Verquickung von Mythos und Geschichte, der Unmöglichkeit einer Ontologie, der Haltlosigkeit aller Anfänge".[10]

Hos neuerer Film *The Cloud of Unknowing* (2011) wurde zuerst im Singapur-Pavillon der Venedig Biennale 2011 präsentiert. In einem verfallenen Block mit verlassenen Wohnungen des Housing Development Board (HDB) in Taman Jurong, einem einkommensschwachen Viertel am äußersten Stadtrand von Singapur, aufgenommen, ist jede der Figuren „obsessiv mit Handlungen beschäftigt, die auf bestehenden Kompositionen aus chinesischen Landschaftsbildern oder westlichen klassischen Gemälden basieren. Gegen Ende des Films steigert sich die Hysterie, da sie von Wolken, Schwaden oder Nebel bedrängt werden. Zuletzt versteht man, dass das, was man für projizierten Rauch gehalten hat, tatsächlich hinter der Leinwand hervortritt.

---

8   Vgl. Charles Lim, *Sea State 2. As Evil Disappears*, sowie das Interview mit Jessica Anne Rahardjo in *ISSUE 1: Land*, Singapur 2012, S. 34–45.
9   David Teh, *Charles Lim's Informatic Naturalism. Notes on Sea State 2*, in: *Sea State 2. As Evil Disappears*, Singapur 2012.
10 Vgl. Ho Tzu Nyen, Forum on Contemporary Art and Society, 2007.

Die Wolke materialisiert sich also."[11] Ho bemerkt weiter: „Für den Film wollte ich diesen bestimmten Block mit seinen düsteren Wohnungen verwenden, weil sie etwas den Wolken völlig Entgegengesetztes sind. Sie sind wie Erde, mit einem Umfeld, das dicht mit gelebter Erfahrung angefüllt ist, mit Alter, mit Erinnerung, mit Verfall."[12] Wie Michelle Lhooq feststellt, „verkörpert die Wolke in ihrer vergänglichen Form den Begriff der Veränderung; ihre Bedeutung in der Erfahrung der Erleuchtung als Vehikel der Erhebung, Grenzmarkierungen einer anderen Welt und Symbol der Transzendenz; und als Übungen für die Imagination, die Leinwand, auf die der Geist projiziert, und als Halluzinationsmaschinen."[13] (s. S. 92)

Zum Schluss möchte ich die Frage beantworten, was das ‚Maß des Wohnens' sei. Durch das Erzählen von Geschichte, von Geschichten und Ereignissen über das Land, Ereignissen aus der Vergangenheit, über Gemeinschaften, die vielfältig sind statt Einheiten – Geschichten und Ereignisse – kann eine vorgestellte Gefahr erkannt werden. Es herrscht eine Angst vor der Kontaminierung der Nation als einheitlicher symbolischer Raum, die die Erfahrung einer unspezifischen Bedrohung hervorruft – das, was das Unheimliche genannt werden kann. In Singapur nimmt das Unheimliche eine besondere Form an. Alle drei Künstler sprengen die Konstruktion eines nationalen Imaginären. Wie sehr die Regierung auch versuchen mag, die Wogen zu glätten, die Geschichte zu einer Geschichte des triumphalen Fortschritts hin zur Gründung der Nation und zur Einheit des singapurischen Volks als Eines zu bereinigen, wird das Unheimliche doch stets auf beunruhigende Weise im Herzen der Heimat anwesend bleiben.

Dezember 2014

---

[11] Michelle Lhooq, *Interview mit Ho Tzu Nyen*, in Interview, Dezember 2014.
[12] Ebd.
[13] Ebd.

UNSETTLING THE PURITY OF ONE

CHARLES MEREWETHER

The title of this project can be taken as a rhetorical phrase that asks the question: what is the measure of one's dwelling? It sketches out the idea of the dwelling place of oneself, the home, the land, and, if you will, the country. And yet, this is not a point of origin,—the fictional narrative of beginnings—a fixed point of determination or reference but rather the space of location. To which the project calls upon the cultural theorist Homi Bhabha's conception of the 'unhomely' as: "an experience in which the sense of safe, private inhabitation is disturbed together with the wider public world, such that both the private and the public become ever stranger and disordered." In so doing Bhabha has expanded the terms of reference in regard to Freud's concept of the 'unheimlich', meaning the unhomely or uncanny for an individual and their personal experience of estrangement from the familiar.[1] This estrangement causes anxiety, transgressing familiar boundaries between the familiar and unfamiliar, boundaries between interiority and exteriority or the private and public. However, in so conceiving Bhabha has also drawn on Derrida in his reading of Freud's concept of 'unheimlich' as based on anxiety.[2] This is an anxiety in which we feel ill at home with ourselves, in a manner that leads to an impending dissolution of our subjectivity.

Bhabha reframes the 'uncanny' in a broader social term of reference, taking as his point of departure the experience of colonialism and forms of resistance by the colonized peoples, drawing also on the literature and cultural work of Edward Said, especially his book *Orientalism* (1978). From this, Bhabha, interjecting on the much-heralded idea of multiculturalism in the 1980's, rewrites its script, enabling

---

[1] See S. Freud, *The Uncanny* (1919) in *The Standard Edition of the Complete Psychological Works of Sigmund Freud*, Volume XVII (1917-1919).
[2] Jacques Derrida, *Archive Fever: A Freudian Impression* (Chicago University Press, 1998).

an exploration of cross-cultural relations between people and ethnicities. Armed with notions of ambivalence, hybridization and mimicry, Bhabha focuses on cultural difference, as distinct from cultural diversity. That is, while cultural diversity is the object of empirical knowledge, cultural difference is discursively constructed by virtue of a process of enunciation. This process is a means of discovery and recognition. This being said what followed from this intervention on the part of Bhabha was an extraordinary wave of writings that rewrote the cultural history of civilizations since the conquest of the Americas more than five hundred years ago. And, while the presence and recognition of hybridity is an achievement, it has not changed its co-option under the sign of cultural diversity and the process of selectivity and assimilation or exclusion.

And yet, how then does this lead to the case of Singapore, a country no more than fifty years old, although enmeshed in a complex history of emergence as a nation in relation to its neighbors Malaysia, Indonesia, India and to China? Moreover, the context of this project is about Singaporean contemporary art practice. What matters here is not the concept of hybridity so much as that of the unhomely.

The degree to which the experience of Singapore weighs heavily on the consciousness of many artists in Singapore is striking. There is a sense of disquiet about belonging to a nation, as if the identity of being Singaporean is profoundly unsatisfactory, to the point of being unsettling. It is not that it means nothing, it means too much! It imposes. But what is it? Perhaps, we may begin by suggesting that it is the weight of a state that seeks to be recognized as a Nation State, as a sovereign power, as a culture that is not an extension of China nor simply another Southeast Asian country. In fact, Singapore seeks to rise above this latter designation in its ambition to represent those countries, as instanced by the ambition of the National Gallery that will open in 2015. The paring down of this complex history into the Singaporean has affected even Parankan peoples whose contemporary and past history has been relegated to the corridors of the historical past and museums. Moreover, the State seeks to regulate the contemporary art scene by virtue of its funding and support. The National Arts Council offers grants and studios to those they deem worthy, especially in recent years, those who celebrate the notion of 'community.' Community Arts is celebrated, whatever, and virtually however this might mean, as long as it is named as such.

Fundamental to the experience of unhomely is the way in which the familiar was made strange, an experience in which domesticity itself was disturbed. As Jason Wee notes: "…the ambivalence experienced by a character connected to 'wider disjunctions of political existence', for one, and for another, a sense of place that obscures or erases itself, through hesitation, deprivation or distance. The exhibition and my essay is a chance for me to shift its emphasis on the literary towards the spatial dimensions of the unhomely—its infrastructure, its urban plan, its built verticality, its organization of our movement, heritage, and site."[3]

---

[3] Jason Wee, Notes for Curatorial Proposal. unpublished. We are reminded of Anthony Vidler who argues that an architectural dimension is embedded within the 'unhomely.' See Anthony Vidler, *The Architectural Uncanny*, (Mass.: MIT Press, 1994).

In a place where the home and domesticity is so central to everyday life, this disturbance seeps into a broader sphere of issues of identity, cultural displacement and exile. Add to this the impact of information technologies on the once secure myth of domestic privacy and the family as a virtual community. The technological network extends the domestic boundaries as mobility itself enters the core of domesticity, affecting the definition of privatization itself.

Latent too within these discussions is the redefinition of community, that is an understanding of community that is neither singular nor confined to that of the home or to nation and all of which these factors imply. For what we speak of here is the sense of belonging that the concept of community implies. Moreover, this communal life is represented as one, a coherence of identity standing for the singularity of nationhood, as of Singapore. This is the moral force of the community as one, it is not the ethics of singularity. Rather, it is the demand for representation (and reproduction) that excludes the idea of community as plural, contestational, as difference. Moreover, as Benedict Anderson so cogently argued in his book *Imagined Communities*,[4] the nation is a symbolic space, whose ideological purity is constructed in response to the anxiety of its contamination. This threat of contamination is the experience of the unhomely or that which threatens to disrupt the imagined security of the homeliness of the community and sovereignty of the nation.

In this overbearing context, artists today in Singapore seek to breathe the air of other cultures. Some artists prefer not be called Singaporean artist, others simply escape, taking a residency that in turn might become a means of extending a stay elsewhere and then others simply travel from station to station, by means of exhibitions and residencies and the hospitality of others. Is what has resulted in this disquiet from artists living in Singapore an exploration of certain disjunctions? To answer this, let me turn back to the moment of 'enunciation' of cultural difference. For this moment opens up a much more volatile environment with the possibility of change, a resistance to or shift away from any stereotyping or fixity or the projection of purity that serves as a homogenizing force unifying community under the sign of a national identity. Following this line of argument, culture is not a pre-given. There is then no certitude in the idea of a traditional or stable point of reference such as the home or State.

Three of the artists chosen for the exhibition are principally working with film or video: Tan Pin Pin, Charles Lim and Ho Tzu Nyen. The extensive practice of each artist is quite distinct from one another but can be brought together as forming critiques of the essentializing process of the State as a sovereign nation through the 'purification' of its history and origins and the ideological construction of 'community.'

In 2001, Tan Pin Pin presented *Moving House*. The short fim addressed the resettlement of some thousands of families after they were forced to move from village communities into modern public housing estates. In many respects, this government policy corresponds to the plight of Chinese families displaced from their traditional hutongs into high rise apartment buildings by the Chinese government.

---

4   Benedict Anderson, *Imagined Communities: Reflections on the Origin and Spread of Nationalism*, (London: Verso, 1983).

The result was the destruction of these communties producing in its palce the typical atomization of modern urban life common in the West. The filmmaker then integrated into her film the account of one of these families who were forced to relocate the remains of their relatives from a cemetery to a columbarium. A tacit parallel was evident.

More recently, Tan made *To Singapore, With Love* (2013) about the plight of six political exiles, all of whom "have different ideological positions and are of different ages; some are communists, others are activists from the Christian Left, yet others are socialist politicians or former student activists."[5] However, it was immediately banned by the Singapore government for "undermining national security."[6] Perhaps the government is right, but perhaps it is not. Its blanket censorship seems counter-productive. In a democracy a public airing would allow for differences of opinion and evalutation based on the evidence to be aired and people to make up their own minds. (s. S. 110)

In 2011 the artist Charles Lim produced a 20-minute video, *All the Lines Flow Out*, which follows the journey of a mysterious figure who walks along the longkangs—a local term for drains—that create a vast network across the city state of Singapore.[7] The figure can be seen as searching for a way home. Recalling the mysterious landscape of Andrei Tarkovsky, Lim creates a mysterious latter-day world of Baudelaire's flaneur. And yet, these longkangs have, over the years, been slowly subsumed the dictates of Singapore's almost compulsive obsession to construct itself as a modern cityscape. This construction ignores the boundless force of nature, evident when the city is immobilised by the monsoon period causing flash flooding that can strike at the heart of its shopping district.

Lim has expanded his view of Singapore to look at its topographical character, discovering that even this is not immune to the governmental logic of instrumentality and its ambition. In a series of short films and installations under the title *Sea State*, Lim explored the nation's physical growth of Singapore through the addition of sand to its shores—land 'reclamation' projects as called—which has involved the dredging of sand from small islands belonging to Indonesia and neighboring countries.[8] This resulted in Singapore being the top of the list of countries that have actually grown in physical size. This activity has subsequently stopped. But in writing of the *Sea State* project, David Teh has suggested that it captures how the

---

5 Tan statement, *Notes from Serangoon Road*, 2014.

6 The Singaporean Minister for Communications and Information, Dr Yaacob said the film "*To Singapore, With Love* contains untruths and deception about this history." He went on to say "To allow the public screening of a film that obfuscates and whitewashes an armed insurrection by an illegal organisation, and violent and subversive acts directed at Singaporeans, would effectively mean condoning the use of violence and subversion in Singapore, and thus harm our national security."

7 The following words on Charles Lim are drawn from a published essay of mine: *Future Imaginaries in Asian Connectivities*, Edited Michelle Antoinette and Caroline Turner. (Canberra: Australian National University), 2014.

8 See Charles Lim, *Sea State 2: As Evil Disappears*, and interview with Jessica Anne Rahardjo, in *ISSUE 1: Land* (Singapore, 2012), 34–45.

'maritime geography' has been 'all but erased from the national imaginary and everyday experience' replaced by land-based urban visions.[9] (s. S. 58)

Ho Tzu Nyen has written of one of his early films *Utama: Every Name in History is I* (2003) that it is "an attempt to summon forth the specter of Utama." In an article published in Forum on Contemporary Art and Society (2007), Ho traces the story of "how cats—big and small, wild and domesticated, imagined and real—have been enigmatically woven into the history of Singapore." Through a combination of mythic legends and historical fact about the founding Singapore, Ho addresses issues around the construction of identity or identity politics in regard to the State and nationbuiding. Ultimately this is a film about "the intertwining of myth and history, the impossibility of ontology, the instability of all beginnings."[10]

More recently Ho has directed *The Cloud of Unknowing* (2011) that was first presented at the Singapore pavilion at the Venice Biennale in 2011. Shot in a decaying block of vacated HDB (Housing Development Board) apartments in Taman Jurong, a low-income area in the remote outskirts of Singapore, each of the characters are "obsessively doing activities based on existing compositions from Chinese landscapes or Western classical paintings. Close to the end of the film, it becomes more hysterical as they're invaded by clouds, vapors, or mist. Finally, what you think is projected smoke you realize is actually coming from behind the screen. So the cloud is materialized."[11] Ho went on note that "For this film I wanted to use this particular block of grimy flats because they're something completely opposite to clouds. They're like earth, with an environment that's dense with lived experience, with age, with memory, with decay."[12] As Michelle Lhooq further suggests the cloud is "embodying in its transient form the notion of change; its signification in the experience of illumination as vehicles of elevation, boundary markers of a different world and symbols of transcendence; and as exercises for the imagination, the screen upon which the mind projects, and engines of hallucination.[13] (s. S. 92)

To conclude, let us respond to the question: 'what is the measure of ones dwelling'. By recounting histories, stories and incidents about the land, events of the past, about communities that are plural, not one—stories and incidents—an imagined threat can be recognized. There is an anxiety of the contamination of the nation as a unified symbolic space which causes the experience of an unspecified threat, that which can be named the unhomely. The unhomely takes on a specificity in Singapore. Each of these three artists disrupt the construction of a national imaginary. However much the government seeks to smooth the waters, to streamline history as one of triumphant progress to nationhood and the unity of the people of Singapore as one, the unhomely will remain an unsettling presence in the heart of the home.

December 2014

9 David Teh, *Charles Lim's Informatic Naturalism: Notes on Sea State 2*, in Sea State 2: As Evil Disappears. (Singapore, 2012).
10 See Ho Tzu Nyen, Forum on Contemporary Art and Society (2007).
11 Michelle Lhooq, interview with Ho Tzu Nyen in Interview magazine, December 2014.
12 ibid.
13 ibid.

THERE IS A SENSE OF DISQUIET ABOUT BELONGING TO A NATION, AS IF THE IDENTITY OF BEING IS PROFOUNDLY UNSATISFACTORY, TO THE POINT OF BEING UNSETTLING.

CHARLES MEREWETHER
"UNSETTLING THE PURITY OF ONE"

SINGAPOREAN

DAS MASS DES WOHNENS: SINGAPUR UNHEIMLICH

JASON WEE

Seit einigen Jahrzehnten ist die Vorstellung, Singapur sei für seine Bewohner ein gastfreundlicher Wohnort auf einer Insel, inzwischen zu einer ebenso kraftvollen Selbstbestätigung für die politische Führung wie sie für die Bürger ein Gegenstand der Sorge geworden ist. Ein Teil dieser Kraft ist die politische Entgegnung auf die Ungewissheit, dass eine unabhängige Inselnation ihre Unabhängigkeit womöglich nicht lange bewahren könne, ein anderer Teil besteht in der Stärkung der zentralen Rolle der Regierung bei der Aufrechterhaltung dieser Unabhängigkeit; seit über einem halben Jahrhundert hält die People's Action Party ununterbrochen die Macht inne. Bezeichnenderweise verbindet sich die Sorge um die Heimat und das Wohnen mit einer Identitätskrise in Bezug auf die Traditionen und das kulturelle Erbe inmitten einer Phase des rasanten Bevölkerungswachstums und des demografischen Wandels; nach offizieller Schätzung wird die Bevölkerung Singapurs in den kommenden fünfzehn Jahren um 40 % anwachsen, während der Anteil der Staatsbürger an der Gesamtbevölkerung von heute 62 % auf 55 % absinken wird.[1] Diese Sorge um die Selbstdefinition weist einige Parallelen zu europäischen Identitätsdebatten auf und umfasst auch Anflüge von nationalistischen Argumenten (von Bürgern dieses überwiegend aus Einwanderern bestehenden Landes) zugunsten wesentlicher Traditionalismen sowie den Anstieg klassenspezifischer Fremdenfeindlichkeit, die sich vorrangig gegen ausländische Arbeiter und Gäste aus den weniger wohlhabenden Schichten der Nachbarländer richtet.

Mit Beginn des Jahres 2015 rücken diese Debatten aus dem Fokus des Interesses, ohne dabei jedoch vollständig abzuklingen. Dieses Jahr ist besonders stark von nationalem Optimismus bis hin zur Überdeterminierung geprägt. Es ist das Jahr des fünfzigsten Jubiläums der Unabhängigkeit von Malaysia, Impetus für alle Arten von Feierlichkeiten im Lande und für die historische Konsolidierung. Für SG50 wurde ein spezieller Fonds geschaffen, um die heimatliche Gastfreundschaft der Insel zu betonen, ein Inselwunder mit einem so überzeugenden Paradies, dass seine Politiker unzählige Wege finden, es zu propagieren. Eine dieser Kampagnen trägt den einfallsreichen Titel *SG Heart Map* und zielt, in den Worten eines Berichts, darauf ab, „einen

---

1   National Population and Talent Division (Singapur), Prime Minister's Office, *A Sustainable Population For A Dynamic Singapore*, Population White Paper, Singapur, Januar 2013.

Bilderteppich der besonderen Orte zu weben, die Singapur als Heimat ausmachen".[2] Die national gesonnene Zeitung The Straits Times hat die Polemik *The Battle for Merger (Der Kampf um die Vereinigung)* von 1962 neu herausgegeben, Abschriften von zwölf Radiogesprächen, die der damalige Premierminister Lee Kuan Yew zugunsten der gescheiterten Vereinigung Singapurs mit Malaysia geführt hatte. Die junge Kunstinstitution National Gallery of Singapore betreibt ihr eigenes SG50-Projekt, mit dem „ganz Singapur zusammengebracht" werden soll, um pflichtbewusst Selbstporträts als feierliche Reflexion über den Treueeid beizutragen, während ein Fußgängerübergang zwischen dem Museum und dem Ausgang einer Unterführung in Jubilee Walk umbenannt wurde. Nichts kann dem Banalen überlassen werden. Für den größten Teil dieses Jahres wird Heimat ein patriotisches Gefühl sein, eine Affirmation der historischen Unausweichlichkeit des Landes, das sogar Infrastrukturflächen wie eine Straßenunterführung in einen feierlichen Dienst verwandelt.

Vor dem Hintergrund dieser Szenerie wird die beharrliche Feier selbst zu einer Sorge, bei der selbst die begeistertsten Unternehmungen mit dem Druck, dies auch mit ausreichender Selbstüberzeugung zu tun, versehen sind. Die Forderung, die Slavoj Žižek in unserer Vergnügungsindustrie identifiziert, nämlich dass „du es mit Vergnügen machen musst. Es muss dir Spaß machen", gilt auch für unsere derzeitige Stimmung, wo unser ambivalenter Wunsch zu feiern sich mit der Vorschrift, dies zu tun, überlagert. Diese Vorschrift gilt nicht nur in diesem Jahr, wenn auch die Intensität größer sein mag. Für den Staat war es politisch wie gesellschaftlich zweckdienlich, wiederholt zur Feier Singapurs aufzufordern und dabei gleichzeitig die ungewisse Zukunft des Landes herauszustellen, die fragile Sicherheit der Nation zu betonen und das Land gleichzeitig aufzurufen, all dessen zu vergöttern, was es gegenwärtig ist.

Die diesem verordneten Jubiläum entsprechende Sorge wird auch durch die Möglichkeit leerer Plattitüden bei der Nachzeichnung der Silhouette dieser Heimat und bei der Bestimmung der Orte, an denen sie aufscheint, hervorgerufen. Die nationalen Kunsteinrichtungen haben bisweilen über diese Lücke reflektiert. In seinem kuratorischen Essay mit dem unironischen Titel *There's No Place Like Home* anlässlich der Ausstellung junger Künstler *Future Proof* (2012) bei 8Q, dem neuen Anbau des Singapore Art Museums, verwertet David Chew erneut den Topos von Singapur als Insel, als Stadt und schließlich als Ort, an dem die „singapurische Identität geschaffen wird."[3] In *At Home Abroad* (2009), einer Ausstellung mit Arbeiten von fünf Künstlern bei 8Q, ist Heimat der simple Kontrapunkt zum Internationalen, der Ausgangs- und letztliche Ankunftspunkt jeder Reise. Die Heimat, die Singapur darstellen soll, erscheint als eine Kluft des ungewissen Werdens, oder als leere Rollbahn.

Die Lücke wird sogar dann sichtbar, wenn der Idee Singapurs auf transnationale Weise nachgegangen wird. In dem Essay der Kunstkritikerin Iola Lenzi für ihre Ausstellung *Negotiating Home, History and Nation* (2011) im Singapore Art Museum, einer Überblicksschau mit Arbeiten aus Südostasien aus zwei Jahrzehnten, erscheint Heimat als eine Ansammlung amorpher Merkmale, die, um Lenzi selbst zu paraphrasieren,

---

2   Amanda Lee, *SG50 search on for what the heart calls home*, in: Today, 15. November 2014, http://www.todayonline.com/singapore/sg50-search-what-heart-calls-home

3   David Chew, Khairuddin Hori (Hg.), *The Singapore Story. Future Proof*, Singapur: Singapore Art Museum, 2012, S. 28 f.

mehr Fragen nach ihrer Politik aufwerfen als sie beantworten. Während die Ausstellung sich energisch vom kolonialen Chauvinismus distanziert, ist für sie Heimat dennoch da, wo die „lokale Würze" zu finden ist, mit all den touristischen Assoziation, die dieser Begriff impliziert.[4] Das „Lokale" wird mit Betonung von „starken Geschichten" und der „Gemeinschaft" ausgewiesen, ohne die offensichtlichen Konnotationen beider Ausdrücke zu hinterfragen und ohne die Ärgernisse und Antagonismen bei der Herstellung von Geschichten oder von Gemeinschaft aufzuzeigen.[5] Auch wenn sich in den Arbeiten der Ausstellung eine große Bandbreite ideologischer Überzeugungen und Forderungen manifestiert, erscheint Heimat als Nation im Kleinen und ist künstlerische Produktion fast immer nur dann „politisch" und insofern für Lenzi exemplarisch, wenn sie als Kontrastfolie gegen das staatliche Dogma steht. Was in diesem Begriff des Politischen fehlt, ist eine Benennung der konkurrierenden Ansprüche und Kontroversen zwischen verschiedenen politischen Strategien um Einfluss oder Wandel. Politik bleibt diesem Verständnis nach auf den Staat konzentriert. Dementsprechend steht Heimat für einen geopolitischen Raum, eine Ansammlung von Nationen, deren konstitutive Nationalismen nicht infrage gestellt werden. In dieser Heimat-Nation wird Lenzis Begriff des Politischen eng gefasst als atomistische Form, in der der Künstler sich direkt an den Staat wendet.

Im Gegensatz dazu möchte ich einen negativen Weg vorschlagen, um den Punkt namens Singapur zu umkreisen, indem man seine schattige Rückseite beobachtet, um ein Maß dieses Wohnens vermittels seiner Unheimlichkeit zu nehmen. In seinem Buch *Die Verortung der Kultur* beschreibt der Literaturkritiker Homi Bhabha die unheimliche Zeit als die Verschränkung „zwischen den traumatischen Ambivalenzen einer persönlichen, psychischen Geschichte und den umfassenderen Brüchen der politischen Existenz", in der die Verwirrungen sich innerhalb eines verborgenen intrapersonellen häuslichen Raumes über seine ungewissen Grenzen zum Öffentlichen und zum Bekannten hinaus auf die größere Welt ausbreiten.[6] Für Bhabha ist der Ort dieser Ausbreitung nicht einfach ein Bruch oder „eine Entzweiung und Aufteilung",[7] sondern auch eine Verbindung, ein Zwischenmoment, wo die Schmerzen des persönlichen Traumas sich wie eine zweite Haut um die Körper legen, ebenso wie der aufflackernde Wunsch nach Solidarität, nach einem ‚sozialen' Leben.

Andeutungsweise kehrt die Verbindung (join) in der architektonischen Beschreibung wieder, nämlich als die etymologische Wurzel einer Konstruktion, die verschiedentlich auch als Schwalbenschwanz, Zapfen oder Gehrung bezeichnet wird. Die Tischlerei (joinery) ist ein Moment der potentiellen und funktionalen Ambivalenz, der Struktur und Ornament, Form und Detail hervorbringt. Vince Ongs *Table #2* lässt sich mit einiger Präzision als gepresste Tischlerei bezeichnen, die ihre Bestandteile entsprechend ihrer größeren und letztgültigen Form in Spannung hält. Zusammen mit einer Skepsis bezüglich der Festigkeit räumlicher Gebilde, offenbaren seine Elemente, die

---

4   Iola Lenzi (Hg.), *Negotiating Home, History and Nation*, Singapur, Singapore Art Museum, 2011, S. 8.
5   Ebd., S. 13–15, 18.
6   Homi K. Bhabha, *Die Verortung der Kultur*, Tübingen: Stauffenberg, 2000, S. 16.
7   Ebd., S. 28.

sich nie in eine geschlossene Einheit auflösen, die Dynamik seiner Strukturierung als Detail und als potentieller Zusammenbruch; ein Nachlassen der Spannung, und der Tisch deformiert sich.

Die Verbindung erlaubt eine Verschiebung von Bhabhas Betonung des Literarischen hin zur räumlichen Dimensionen des Unheimlichen, darauf, wo diese Ambivalenzen verortet, produziert, organisiert werden, darauf, wie diese Ambivalenzen den Raum verorten, produzieren, organisieren. Wenn das Unheimliche, wie der Kurator Okwui Enwezor beschreibt, eine Folge von „Phantomszenen" ist, in denen wir „Entstellungen, Fehler und regelrechte Antagonismen"[8] beobachten, dann richtet *Das Maß des Wohnens* szenografische Aufmerksamkeit auf die Infrastruktur der Insel, auf ihre Stadtplanung, ihre Konfiguration von Bewegungen, Biomasse, Erbe und Ort, um zu beobachten, wie unsere Räume nicht nur den leeren Hintergrund darstellen, auf dem die Fehler und Entstellungen zu finden sind, sondern selbst entstellt und Gegenstand eines Antagonismus werden.

Diese Antagonismen stehen im Widerstreit zu den verbreiteten Erscheinungsformen des Kosmopolitismus in unseren Dörfern und Städten, der nicht als nachträgliche Deutung der gebauten Umgebung erscheint, sondern sich im Bauen als andauernde Handlung manifestiert, in der Konstruktion von Geschäftsvierteln und Schlafstädten, Gated Communities und Gettos, Freihandelszonen und Slums. Nach dieser Lesart wandelt sich die gebaute Materialität unserer vertrauten Wohnorte von physischer Stasis zu gegenwärtiger Volatilität, und Heimat wird zu einem Ereignis, das jenen Moment bezeichnet, in dem wir sie neu verorten. Wohnen und Heimat sind nicht mehr enge Umgrenzungen unseres Privatlebens, sondern eine Sphäre der öffentlichen Auseinandersetzung um widerstreitende Ansprüche in Bezug auf Wohnen, Eigentum und Versorgung. Heimat als Prozess der un-heimlichen Neueinrichtung, als andauernde Ersetzung ihrer selbst zu verstehen, bedeutet in den Worten der Kunsthistorikerin Jennifer Johung, „sich den Momenten und den Orten der Fundierung zuzuwenden […], wo die Bedingungen der räumlichen Situation durch spezifische grundlegende Verhandlungen zwischen Mobilität und Stasis abgesteckt werden."[9]

Die sechs Orte in Tan Pin Pins Film *The Impossibility of Knowing* werden in langen ungeschnittenen Einstellungen eingefangen, die eine Form des zeitlichen Erkennens sind, eine Anerkennung ungesehener Möglichkeiten, die über den betrachteten Ort hinausgehen. Die Orte sind, wie wir im Laufe der Zeit erfahren, Orte des Traumas; an einem von ihnen sprang ein Liebespaar von einem Wohnturm gemeinsam in den Tod; an einem anderen starb ein Mensch alleine und wurde zum Skelett, bevor er gefunden wurde. In ihrer Beschreibung des Films sagt Tan, dass ihre „Kamera nichts ‚eingefangen' hat", doch die Entleerung des Sichtbaren, die von diesem „nichts" angedeutet wird, entstellt unseren Sinn des Gewöhnlichen, während wir die Aufmerksamkeit innerhalb dieser langen Zeitdauer auf deplatzierte Dinge richten. Der Platz selbst ist deplatziert, unvereinbar mit seinen Geschichten, eine zurückgelassene Nut, die mit keinem Zapfen einer Erinnerung verbunden ist.

8   Okwui Enwezor, *BIACS. The Unhomely, Phantom Scenes in Global Society*, Bom, BIACS, 2006, S. 14.
9   Jennifer Johung, *Replacing Home*, Minneapolis: University of Minnesota Press, 2012, S. 21.

Ein Platz, der mit sich selbst im Konflikt steht, kann eine gute Beschreibung für einen Zustand des inneren Exils sein, der die Entfernung zwischen dem Inneren und dem Äußeren eines Ortes ‚innerhalb' dieses Ortes markiert, wo die Lücke zwischen dem, der willkommen ist, und dem, der fremd ist, sich als innerer Bruch öffnet. Die notdürftigen Unterkünfte und Häuserreihen in Chua Chye Tecks Fotoreihe *Paradise* beschwören ein unheimliches Gespenst von Armut und Entbehrung herauf, trotz Chuas Vorstellung, dass sie nicht für die oder von den Obdachlosen gemacht sind. Während sie von Chua als Zuflucht beschrieben werden, ähneln sie auch einer ‚entfremdenden' (othering) Architektur des Exils und der Flucht, das heißt des Flüchtlings. Der Rückzug von dem Blick der Stadt, begrenzt von ihren Orten innerhalb des engen Küstenstreifens von Punggol, markiert eine entlegene Zone der Abweichung[10] von der geplanten Entwicklung, eine Abweichung mit starker Entsprechung zu der Distanz zwischen der glitzernden Metropole der Gegenwart und einer bescheideneren Vergangenheit, eine Distanz, die sich, um einen schroffen Vergleich zu gebrauchen, in der größer werdenden wirtschaftlichen Ungleichheit zwischen jenen spiegelt, die Geld machen, und jenen, die im Leben zurechtkommen. Diese Architektur des Zurechtkommens mit den rudimentären Notwendigkeiten der Unterkunft begründet eine Entfremdung von der Ursache der Gentrifizierung und Verdichtung. Doch statt des Rückzugs in eine haltlose Sehnsucht nach vergangener Einfachheit lassen diese armseligen Konstruktionen das Bild der glänzenden Stadt als fremd erscheinen, indem sie Raum für das Heterogene, das Unbeständig-Gemachte schaffen.

Die Verfremdung in Zai Tangs *Respect* ist zweifältig: Erstens ist die Schallplatte eine Pressung von Außenaufnahmen, die auf dem Friedhof Bukit Brown gemacht wurden, ein 86 Hektar großes Zeugnis in Form von Gräbern von der frühen Einwandererwelle auf das Archipel, auf dem Singapur liegt, ein Zeugnis, das aufgrund von Plänen für eine Autobahn bald verschwunden sein wird. Zweitens nutzt sich die Schallplatte mit jedem Gebrauch in der Ausstellung ab, mit jedem Mal, dass sie abgespielt wird, verschleißt die Rille, in die die Töne eingraviert sind, bis zur endgültigen Entropie. Die Außenaufnahmen verklingen, wie als Echo des letztendlichen Schicksals des Friedhofs, nur kurz nach der ersten Entdeckung durch ihre Zuhörer in ewigem Rauschen. Hier ist Geschwindigkeit von wesentlicher Bedeutung; die Entropie beginnt, sobald wir uns mit dem Klang und dem Ort vertraut machen. Sowohl bei der Friedhofsstätte wie bei den Aufnahmen ist die Kenntnis des Ortes zusammen mit der Intimität seiner klanglichen Wirkungen mit der Beteiligung – wie passiv sie auch sein mag – an dem Verfall dieses Wissens verquickt.

Das fremd gemachte Häusliche, wie man es in frühen Beschreibungen des Unheimlichen findet, existiert im Haus, das, wie Anthony Vidler bemerkt, der *locus suspectus* des Unheimlichen ist,[11] das heimgesuchte Gebiet des Nichtsprechenden und des Unaussprechlichen. Das Häusliche ist ein doppelter Grund: der der Inkarnation des Vertrauten wie der Distanzierung davon; hier finden Auslöschung, Verdrängung und andere gewaltsame Akte statt, spielt sich jedoch auch das Unaussprechliche ab.

---

10   Michel Foucault, *Andere Räume*, in: Karlheinz Barck u.a. (Hg.), *Aisthesis. Wahrnehmung heute oder Perspektiven einer anderen Ästhetik*, Leipzig: Reclam, 1992, S. 34–46.

11   Anthony Vidler, *The Architectural Uncanny. The Unhomely Homes of the Romantic Sublime*, in: Assemblage, Nr. 3 (Juli 1987), S. 12.

In Geraldine Kangs Fotografien *Of Two Bedrooms* ist die Sozialwohnung in purem Weiß gehalten, nicht zufällig die Farbe sowohl der chinesischen Trauerkleidung wie der Singapurer Regierungspartei. Zwei Betten, auf denen einst zwei verschiedene Frauen lagen, stehen nun leer nebeneinander. Die Kamera fängt eine Reflexion ein, die die Frage danach, ‚wer sieht', auf morbide Weise verstummen lässt. Eine brennende Fußmatte stört die monochrome Ruhe in einem Augenblick des geisterhaften Abschieds und des schreckenerregenden Willkommens.

Mit diesen und anderen Werken geben die beteiligten Künstler und Autoren verschiedene Antworten auf Singapur als „Problem-Raum", um Enwezors Beschreibung (die wiederum von David Scott stammt) zu übernehmen,[12] als eine Szene, in die das Unheimliche eine schattenhafte Störung einbringt. Die Störung ist Zeichen eines Heimgesucht-Werdens, eines wiederkehrenden Risses, ein Zeichen der verborgenen und der unterdrückten Durchstiche ins Sichtbare. Entscheidend ist, dass ein Problem-Raum einen Kontext für die Identifizierung des Einsatzes der Argumentation, der Vorschläge und Streitfragen entfaltet. Die Ausstellung *Die Vermessung deiner Wohnung* stellt sich selbst als Problem-Raum dar, der Bedingungen und Begriffe anbietet, nicht um die Meinungen über diesen Flecken Land zu verfestigen, sondern um ihn sich zukünftig mit ihm kritisch auseinanderzusetzen.

---

12   Enwezor, a.a.O., S. 15.

THE MEASURE OF YOUR DWELLING:
SINGAPORE AS UNHOMED

JASON WEE

For some decades now, the idea of Singapore as a hospitable island dwelling for its inhabitants is as much a forceful self-assertion by its leaders as it is a matter of anxiety for its citizens. Part of that force is a political counter against the uncertainty that an independent island nation may not survive its independence long, and part of it is a government reinforcing its centrality in ensuring that independence; the People's Action Party has held uninterrupted power in Singapore for over half a century. Significantly, the anxiety around home and dwelling coalesces around an identity crisis over its traditions and culture amidst rapid population growth and demographic changes; by an official projection, the population of Singapore will grow by 40 % over the next fifteen years, with citizenry narrowing from the present 62 % to 55 % of total residents.[1] This anxiety over self-definition bears some parallels with European identitarian debates, with shades of nativist arguments (by citizens of this largely immigrant country) in favor of essentializing traditionalisms, and the rise of class-specific xenophobia directed primarily at migrant workers and visitors from less-affluent strata of neighboring countries.

These debates, without fully abating, fall out of the spotlight as 2015 arrives. As years go, this year is particularly heavy with national optimism, to the point of overdetermination. It is the fiftieth anniversary of its independence from Malaysia, and the impetus to all manner of domestic celebration and historical consolidation. A special SG50 fund has been set up to emphasize the island's homely welcome, an island wonder with a paradise so compelling its politicians find myriad ways to propound it. One such campaign is the imaginatively titled *SG Heart Map* which, in the words of one report, "aims to weave a tapestry of the special places that define Singapore as home."[2] The nation-building newspaper The Straits Times has reissued

---

[1] National Population and Talent Division (Singapore), Prime Minister's Office, A *Sustainable Population For A Dynamic Singapore*, Population White Paper. Singapore, January 2013.

[2] Amanda Lee, *SG50 search on for what the heart calls home*, in: Today, 15. November 2014, http://www.todayonline.com/singapore/sg50-search-what-heart-calls-home

the 1962 polemic *The Battle for Merger,* transcripts of twelve radio talks given by then—Prime Minister Lee Kuan Yew in favor of Singapore's failed merger with Malaysia. The new art institution National Gallery of Singapore has a SG50 project of its own, to 'rally all of Singapore' to contribute self-portraits as their dutifully solemn reflection on the pledge of allegiance, while a pedestrian walkway between the gallery and a subway exit has been rebranded a Jubilee Walk. Nothing can be left to the ordinary. Home for much of this year will be a patriotic sentiment, an affirmation of the country's historical inevitability that presses even infrastructural spaces like a subway connector into celebratory service.

Set against this scene, insistent celebration becomes its own anxiety, coloring even the most ardent attempts with the pressure to do it with sufficient self-belief. What Slavoj Žižek identifies within our pleasure industries, a demand that insists "you must do it with pleasure. You must enjoy it" can be said of our current sentiment, that our ambivalent desire to celebrate overlaps with an injunction to do so. The injunction is not peculiar to the year, though the intensity of it may be. It was political and socially expedient for the state to repeatedly call for a celebration of Singapore while at the same time emphasizing its future uncertainty, emphasizing the fragile security of the nation while calling on the country to lionize whatever it presently is.

The corresponding anxiety to this injunctive jubilee is induced as well by the possibility of empty platitudes when delineating the silhouette of this home, and specifying the sites of its appearances. The national art institutions have at times reflected this lacuna. In his curator's essay unironically titled *There's No Place Like Home,* for the young-artist showcase *Future Proof* (2012) at 8Q, the newer art annex of the Singapore Art Museum, David Chew recycles the topes of Singapore as island, as city, and finally as the place where "the Singapore identity is in the making."[3] In *At Home Abroad* (2009), an exhibition of works by five artists at 8Q, home is the simple counterpoint to the international, the point of departure and eventual arrival of any travel. The home that Singapore is meant to be appears as a gap of uncertain becoming, or an empty runway.

The lacuna appears even when the idea of Singapore is pursued transnationally. In the essay by art writer Iola Lenzi for her exhibition *Negotiating Home, History and Nation* (2011) at the Singapore Art Museum, a survey of works from Southeast Asia over two decades, home appears as a cluster of amorphous characteristics that, to paraphrase Lenzi's own words, ask more questions of her politics than answer them. While strenuously distancing the exhibition from colonial chauvinism, home is nonetheless where 'local flavor' is found, with all the touristic associations that term implies.[4] The 'local' is signposted with emphasis on 'strong stories' and 'the community', without questioning the self-evident framing of either terms, or revealing the vexations and antagonisms within either the making of story or community.[5] Though works in the exhibition manifest a range of ideological commitments and claims,

---

3   David Chew, Khairuddin Hori, eds. *The Singapore Story: Future Proof.* Singapore: Singapore Art Museum, 2012, 28-29.
4   Iola Lenzi, ed. *Negotiating Home, History and Nation.* Singapore, Singapore Art Museum, 2011, 8.
5   Ibid, 13-15, 18.

home appears as the nation writ small, and artistic production is almost always only 'political', and thereby exemplary for Lenzi, when it stands as a foil against state dogma. Absent from this notion of the political is any description of competing claims and contestations between different polities for influence or change. Politics, in this sense, defaults to the state-centric. Consequently, home stands as a geopolitical space, an aggregation of nations in which the constitutive nationalisms are unchallenged.. In this nation-as-home, Lenzi's political is narrowly conceived as an atomistic mode of direct address by an artist towards the state.

Against this, I suggest a negative path, to circle the dot that is Singapore by tracing its shadow face, to take a measure of this dwelling by its un-homeliness. In his volume *The Location of Culture*, the literary critic Homi Bhabha describes an unhomely time as the refraction of "the traumatic ambivalences of a personal, psychic history to the wider disjunctions of political existence," in which the perplexities within a hidden, intrapersonal domestic realm spill past its uncertain boundary with the public and the known, onto the wider world.[6] For Bhabha, the loci of the spill is not simply a break or "a sundering and splitting"[7] but also a join, an interstitial moment where the aches of personal trauma press as close as skin, as well as the flickering desire for solidarity, for a 'social' life.

Suggestively, the join recurs in architectural description, as the etymological root for a construction that is also variously termed the dovetail, the mortise, the miter. Joinery is a moment of potential and functional ambivalence, occasioning support and ornament, form and detail. Vince Ong's *Table #2* can be described with some accuracy as extruded joinery that holds in tension its constituents apposite its larger and final form. In tandem with a skepticism about the fixity of spatial formations, its elements, never resolving into a closed unity, expose the dynamics of its structuration as detail and as potential collapse; a slack in the tension and the table deforms.

The join permits a shift of Bhabha's emphasis on the literary towards the spatial dimensions of the unhomely, to where these ambivalences are located, produced, organized, to how these ambivalences produce, locate, organize space. If the unhomely is as the curator Okwui Enwezor describes, a sequence of "phantom scenes" where we observe "disfigurations, lapses and outright antagonisms",[8] *The Measure Of Your Dwelling* brings a scenographic attention to the island's infrastructure, its urban plan, its configuration of movement, biomass, heritage and place, to observe how our spaces are not just the vacant backdrops upon which these lapses and disfigurations are found, but are themselves disfigured and antagonized.

These antagonisms contend with the prevailing manifestations of cosmopolitanism in our towns and cities, where cosmopolitanism appears not as a postfactum reading of the built environment, but materializes in building as ongoing action, in the constructing of business districts and commuter towns, gated communities and ghettoes, tax-free zones and slums. In this emphasis, the built materiality of our intimate

---

6   Homi Bhabha, *The Location of Culture*. London: Routledge, 1994, 11-12.
7   Ibid, 18.
8   Okwui Enwezor, *BIACS: The Unhomely, Phantom Scenes in Global Society*. Bom: BIACS, 2006, 14.

habitations shifts from physical stasis to present volatility, when home becomes an event describing that moment in which we re-place its location. Dwelling and home are no longer tight enclosures of private lives, but a sphere of public contention around conflicting claims of residency, property and care. To think of home as a process of unhomely revisitation, of ongoing replacement of iself, is in the words of the art historian Jennifer Johung to 'attend to the moments and sites of grounding … where the conditions for spatial situation are conceived through specific material negotiations between mobility and stasis.'[9]

The six locations in Tan Pin Pin's film *The Impossibility of Knowing* are captured in long single shots that are a form of durational recognition, an acknowledgement of unseen possibilities that exceeds the place in view. The locations, as we come to learn, are sites of trauma; at one, a pair of lovers jumped to their deaths from a residential tower; another, where a person died alone, living a skeleton to be discovered. Tan in her film synopsis says that (her) camera did not 'capture' anything, yet the evacuation of the visible suggested by that 'anything' disfigures our sense of the ordinary as we pay attention, within these long durations, to things out of place. Place itself is out of place, irreconcilable to its histories, a vacated mortise unintegrated with the tenon of any recollection.

A place at odds with itself may well describe a condition of internal exile, that marks the distance between the inside and outside of a place within that place, where the gap between the welcomed and the stranger opens as an inner fracture. The makeshift shelters and terraces in Chua Chye Teck's photo series *Paradise* raise an uncanny spectre of poverty and privation, despite Chua's belief that they are not made by or for the homeless. While they are described by Chua as refuge, they also resemble an 'othering' architecture of exile and escape, that is, of the refugee. The escape from sight of the city, delimited by their locations within Punggol's narrow coastal belt, designates an outlying zone of deviation[10] from planned development, a deviation with much equivalence to the distance between the glittering metropolis of the present and a humbler past, a distance mirrored by the widening economic inequalities, to use a blunt comparison, between those who are making dough and those making do. This architecture of making do, of getting by with the rudimentary essentials for shelter, grounds an estrangement from the reason of gentrification and densification. Yet, rather than a withdrawal into an unfounded nostalgia for past simplicity, these poor constructions defamiliarize the image of the shining city by making room for the heterogeneous, the unsteadily-made.

The defamiliarization in Zai Tang's *Respect* is two-fold: first, the dubplate is a pressing of field recordings made within Bukit Brown cemetery, a 213-acre burial record of the early diasporic waves to the archipelago that Singapore is embedded in, a record soon to be disappeared by highway expansion plans. Second, the dubplate degrades with each exhibited use, each playback wearing away the groove on which the sounds are etched, until the point of final entropy. The field recordings,

9   Jennifer Johung, *Replacing Home*, Minneapolis: University of Minnesota Press, 2012, 21.
10   Michel Foucault, *Of Other Spaces*, translated by Jay Miskowiec. Originally published in Architecture, Mouvement, Continuité 5 (1984): 46-4. Public domain. Accessed at http://foucault.info//documents/heterotopia/foucault.heterotopia.en.html. 20 December 2014.

echoing the cemetery's eventual fate, fade into irredeemable noise not long after their listeners' first discovery. Here, speed is crucial; entropy sets in as soon as we begin familiarizing ourselves with sound and place. With both the cemetery site and the recordings, the knowledge of place along with the intimacy of its aural affects is entangled with participation, however passive, in the degradation of that knowledge.

The defamiliarized domestic as found in the early descriptions of the unheimlich is in the house, which, as Anthony Vidler points out, is the *locus suspectus* of the unhomely,[11] the haunted grounds of the unspeaking and the unspeakable. The domestic is a doubled ground, of the instantiation of the familiar and of the distantiation from it; where erasure, repression and other violences occur, yet also where the unspeakable is unspooled. In Geraldine Kang's *Of Two Bedrooms* photographs, the public housing flat is bare white, not by accident the color of both Southern Chinese funerary clothing and Singapore's ruling party. Two beds, once laid upon by two different women, now lay empty side by side. The camera catches a reflection that leaves the question of 'who sees' morbidly mute. A burning doormat unsettles the monochrome tranquility in a moment of spectral farewell, and of terrifying welcome.

With these works and others, the participating artists and writers elaborate various responses to Singapore as 'problem-space', to borrow Enwezor's description (itself borrowed from David Scott),[12] as a scene into which the unhomely introduces a shadowy disturbance. The disturbance is a sign of a haunting, of a recurring fissure, of the hidden and the repressed puncturing into the visible. Crucially, a problem-space unfolds a context for identifying the stakes for argumentation, propositions and contestations. Together with its exhibition, reading room and film program, *The Measure Of Your Dwelling* offers itself as a problem-space that offers terms and grounds, not for consolidating opinions about this dot of a country, but for its future disputation.

---

11   Anthony Vidler, *The Architectural Uncanny: The Unhomely Homes of the Romantic Sublime*, Assemblage No. 3 (July 1987), 12.

12   Enwezor, ibid, 15.

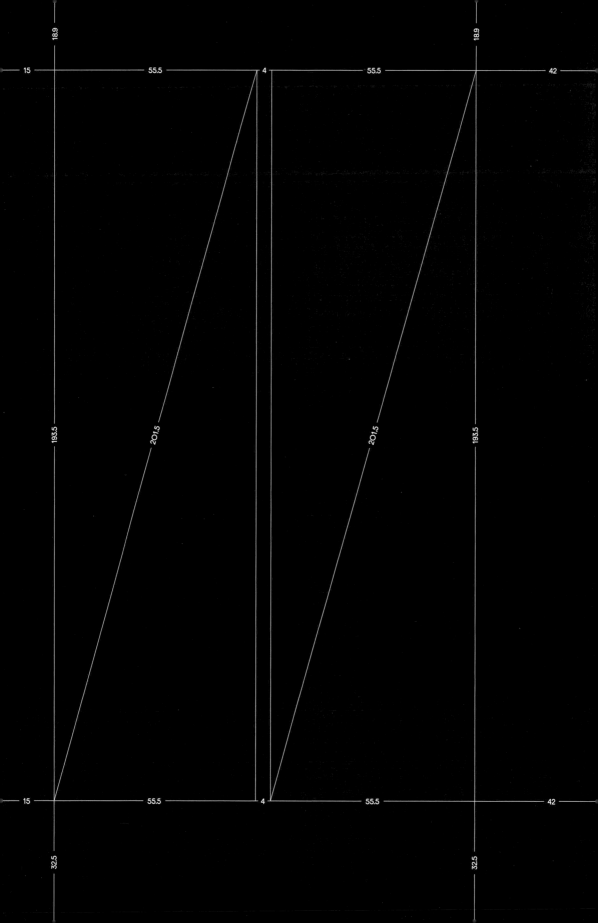

ASHLEY YEO

IM GESPRÄCH MIT GREGORY COATES,
KÜNSTLER UND FRÜHERER TUTOR

Gregory Coates (G.C.): Ashley, beim Betrachten deiner Arbeiten und Bilder scheint mir eine Verbindung zum Innen- und Außenraum zu bestehen. Meine erste Frage wäre daher: Was bedeutet für dich der innere und der äußere Raum?

Ashley Yeo (A.Y.): Der innere als privater / der äußere als öffentlicher Raum. In keinem von beiden ist es angenehmer als im anderen, da die Menschen zwischen diesen beiden verschiedenen Räumen leben. Mich interessieren die narrativen Werte von Räumen und wie die Individuen sie wahrnehmen. Als physische Räume bieten sie den Betrachtern zugleich eine Plattform, um sich zwischen dem kontemplativen und dem narrativen Raum zu bewegen, während sie die Arbeit erfahren. Der innere Raum bietet für mich Trost. Beruhigend, privat, still – meiner. Der äußere Raum hingegen erinnert mich an Weite, an die Erhabenheit der Natur, aber auch an Angst und Lärm, Gedrängtheit; an Extrovertiertheit, Energie.

G.C. In deinen Arbeiten entdecke ich eine filigrane und doch mutige Emotionalität; wann hast du dir selbst ‚erlaubt', dich durch deine Kunst zu offenbaren?

A.Y. Mich interessiert das Emotionale und die Innerlichkeit, auch wenn ich sie nicht zu definieren versuche. Ein Großteil meiner Arbeit entspringt einer Sehnsucht und einem Mangel. Ich war immer ein sanfter Mensch, allzu verletzlich und übersensibel. Das ist auch der Grund, weshalb ich Arbeiten mache, die Zeit benötigen, da mich das entschleunigt, wodurch wiederum meine Gedanken zur Ruhe kommen.

Ich fühle mich zur ‚saudade' hingezogen sowie zum Pathos der Dinge. Ich versuche, meinen Zeichnungen diese Eigenschaften zu verleihen, auch wenn ich mich in letzter Zeit frage, ob überhaupt etwas Inneres übrig bleibt, da jeder verletzlich ist. Eigentlich vermeide ich es, den privaten Kontext in meine Arbeiten aufzunehmen, und ich arbeite mit isolierten oder riesigen Szenen. Auch wenn die Arbeit an meinen Werken meistens zu einer Art der Bewältigung geworden ist, sodass sie für mich natürlich persönlich sein muss. Mich zu ‚offenbaren' habe ich bewusst vermieden, ich fürchte mich vor dem Narzissmus des Künstlers.

G.C. In deiner Arbeit lässt sich die ‚Hand' der Künstlerin unmöglich übersehen. Und deine Hand ist ganz außergewöhnlich. Was bedeutet das für dich im Bereich der bildenden Kunst tätig zu sein, mit anderen Worten, aus deinen Gedanken wirkliche Dinge ‚herzustellen', statt als Dichterin oder Schriftstellerin zu arbeiten? Kurz, wofür in deinem Leben möchtest du erinnert werden?

A.Y. Vielen Dank! Ich schätze, der Akt des Herstellens drängt sich mir einfach als natürlich auf. Selbstverständlich läuft der Prozess nicht von selbst ab, er ist schwirig und bisweilen ein Kampf. Kunst ist wirklich schwirig. Doch im Augenblick dreht sich mein Leben um das Herstellen von Kunst und das Nachdenken über sie. Ich beziehe mich auf Haruki Murakamis literarische Arbeiten, ihm ist es so außerordentlich gut gelungen, Erzählungen in Worte einzufangen und Geschichten aufzulösen, er hat sie vollendet, und dennoch bleiben die Leser neugierig auf das Ungeschriebene. Die Atmosphären, die er durch seine Worte erschaffen hat, sind gleichzeitig aus einer anderen Welt, beunruhigend, melancholisch und einsam, und doch können seine Geschichten für uns tröstlich sein. Das ist sehr merkwürdig und sehr reizvoll für mich. Auch mit Worten kann es immer noch Mehrdeutigkeit geben. Was ich sagen will, ist, dass es mir wahrscheinlich egal ist: ob Künstlerin, Dichterin, Schriftstellerin. Die Werke verwenden unterschiedliche Sprachen; sie haben eine unterschiedliche Intelligenz (visuelle, räumliche Intelligenz, Koordination von Hand, Geist und Auge im Gegensatz zur artikulierten, verbalen Intelligenz, dem Vokabular, der Fähigkeit, immaterielle Gedanken präzise in Wörter zu übersetzen). Und doch sind die Arbeiten das Ergebnis von großer Sorgfalt und großer Mühe. Ich denke nicht darüber nach, wie ich erinnert werden will. Das ist für mich nicht wichtig. Ich bin eher am Leben interessiert; richtig zu leben, das ist auch schon ziemlich schwierig. Die Welt ist zu groß; ich bin zu klein. Doch das macht mir nichts aus.

ASHLEY YEO IN CONVERSATION WITH
GREGORY COATES, ARTIST AND EX-TUTOR

Gregory Coates (G.C.): Ashley, after looking at your works and images, I feel a connection with interior and exterior space. Question 1: What does interior and exterior space mean to you?

Ashley Yeo (A.Y.): Interior as private / exterior as public space. Neither one is more nor less comfortable as people exist between these two various spaces. I am interested in the narrative values of spaces and how individuals perceive them. At the same time, as physical spaces, they offer a platform for the viewer to revel between contemplative and narrative space as they experience the work. Interior space is of solace to me. Comforting, private, silent; mine. In contrast, the exterior reminds me of vastness, of the sublimity of nature and yet also of anxiety and noise, crowdedness; extroversion, energy.

G.C. Ashley, I felt a delicate and yet bold emotional quality in your work. When did you give yourself 'permission' to expose yourself through your art?

A.Y. I am interested in the emotional and intrinsic though I do not try to define them. A lot of my works stem from longing and absence. I have always been a soft person, bruised too easily and overly sensitive. This is also why I make works that require time, as it slows myself down and in return calms my thoughts.

I am attracted to 'saudade', and towards the pathos of things. I work for my drawings to hold those qualities, though recently I am questioning if there is anything intrinsic left as everyone is hurting. I actually avoid including personal context in my works and work with isolated or vast scenes. Though making my works has usually become a coping mechanism, so that it naturally had to be personal to me. 'Exposure' was something I avoided consciously, I am afraid of the artist's narcissism.

G.C. Ashley, in your work, I can't help but respect the Artist 'Hand' in the creation of the works. And your Hand is exceptional. What does it mean to you to be in the visual arts, in other words to make actual things from your thoughts rather than be a poet or perhaps a writer. So in short, what would you like to be remembered for in your life?

A.Y. Thank you! I suppose the act of making is simply something I think of quite naturally, of course the process does not come naturally, it's difficult and at times a struggle. Art is really difficult. Yet, my life right now revolves around art making and thinking. Using Haruki Murakami's works as literary references, he has so successfully captured narratives in words and resolved stories, had concluded it, while still leaving readers very curious about the unwritten. The atmospheres he has woven through his words are at once otherworldly, unsettling, melancholic and lonely, but we can be comforted through his stories which is very odd and attractive to me. Even through words, there can still be ambiguity. My point is, I suppose it doesn't matter to me: artists, poets, writers. The works are in different languages; of different intelligence (visual, spatial intelligence, hand, mind and eye coordination as opposed to articulate, verbal intelligence, vocabulary, the talent to translate intangible thoughts to words accurately). The works still result from a lot of care and pain. I do not think about being remembered. That doesn't really concern me. I am more interested in living; to live properly, that is also quite difficult. The world is too big; I am too small. That does not bother me though.

Ashley Yeo, *Bones of a Dying World* (*Knochen einer sterbenden Welt*), 2014, pencil on paper (Bleistift auf Papier), 38x56 cm

Ashley Yeo, *A lot of Things are Beyond Me (Vieles ist für mich unbegreiflich)*, 2015, pencil on paper (Bleistift auf Papier), 29x30 cm

Ashley Yeo, *Post Grieving (Nach der Trauer)*, 2013, graphite on paper (Graphit auf Papier), 56x60 cm

Ashley Yeo, *Bones of a Dying World (Knochen einer sterbenden Welt)*, 2013, graphite on paper (Graphit auf Papier), 37x58 cm

CHARLES LIM

ÜBER MEIN VIDEO

All the lines flow out untersucht den Machtkampf des Menschen mit der Natur. Das Werk beginnt in der Regenwasserkanalisation Singapurs, dessen Ausmaß die menschlichen Versuche der Eindämmung und der Kontrolle zeigt, aber der Verfall, der durch das tropische Klima verursacht wird, legt die grundlegende Unmöglichkeit offen, die Natur zu kontrollieren.

Letzten Endes wird der Zuschauer in den Ozean hinaus gespült und ist mit Wasser als reiner Kraft konfrontiert, ohne Gedanken oder Gewissen.

ABOUT   MY   VIDEO

All the lines flow out explores man's power struggle with nature. The work begins in the storm drains of Singapore, whose scale shows man's attempts at containment and control, but the decay caused by the tropical climate hints at the essential impossibility of controlling nature.

Ultimately the viewer is swept out into the ocean and confronts water as pure force, without thought or conscience.

Charles Lim, *All the Lines Flow Out (Alle Linien zerfließen)*, 2011, video still, 21 min

CHUA CHYE TECK

IM GESPRÄCH MIT TRICIA LIM,
KÜNSTLERIN UND KUNSTPÄDAGOGIN

Tricia Lim (T.L.): Woher stammt dein fotografischer Stil und wie hast du ihn gefunden?

Chye Teck (C.T.): Bevor ich Fotograf wurde, war ich Bildhauer. Um meine Skulpturen nach ihrer Fertigstellung zu dokumentieren, nutzte ich die Fotografie in ihrer einfachsten Form. Mein Ziel war, die Kunstwerke so getreu wie möglich aufzunehmen und zu präsentieren; der fotografische Stil war also alles andere als originell, sondern einfach eine zweidimensionale Reproduktion des dreidimensionalen Originals.

Als ich bei meinen täglichen Spaziergängen auf verschiedene Objekte traf, verfolgte ich hier instinktiv dieselbe Herangehensweise, das heißt, ich nutzte die Kamera als Werkzeug, um das Objekt so unverfälscht wie möglich einzufangen. In diesen Gegenständen erkenne ich eine Schönheit und betrachte sie als individuelle Kunstwerke, und darum fotografiere ich sie auch auf die gleiche Weise.

Die Düsseldorfer Schule der Fotografie praktiziert einen sehr ähnlichen Ansatz, und es bestehen zweifellos Ähnlichkeiten, was den Sinn für Objektivität angeht, den Respekt für das ursprüngliche Sujet usw., doch während die Bechers von einem ästhetischen Format ausgingen (Bauwerke einer spezifischen Industrie, ähnliche Formen oder Gestalten, die zu Gruppen zusammengestellt wurden usw.), hat sich bei mir das Format der Multiples aus dem Stil des Aufnehmens und Dokumentierens entwickelt.

T.L. Ja, du scheinst bevorzugt in Form eines seriellen Sammelns zu arbeiten – woher weißt du, wann du aufhören musst?

C.T. Auch wenn es organisch begonnen hat, habe ich schließlich unbewusst verstanden, dass sich ein Überblick im fotografischen Sinne am besten in Form einer Sammlung präsentieren lässt. Wir können klarer erkennen, welche Ähnlichkeiten und Unterschiede in der Form der Objekte bestehen, und auch, was am selben Ort, aber zu verschiedenen Zeiten geschieht. Selbst bei einer Nahaufnahme integriere ich üblicherweise immer auch einen Teil der Landschaft in mein Bild. Wenn ich der Meinung bin, genügend Bilder zu haben, um einen bestimmten Blickpunkt zu präsentieren, dann höre ich auf.

Bei *Paradise* habe ich zehn Jahre gebraucht, um all diese Konstruktionen zu finden und sie zu dokumentieren. Ich habe aufgehört, weil das Gelände, das ich dokumentierte, schrittweise in einen Erholungspark umgewandelt wurde und die Behausungen schlichtweg nicht mehr existierten. Stell dir vor, wie ich zufällig auf die erste Behausung stieß – ich fand das so interessant, dass es mich dazu motivierte, nach weiteren zu suchen: Wie machen es andere Menschen, auf die gleiche

Weise oder anders? Damit begann der Aufbau meiner Sammlung von individuellen ‚Objekten' als kollektive umfassende Idee. Das Thema entspricht auch meinem anhaltenden Interesse an der Erinnerung und dem Verlust oder dem Verschwinden unserer Landschaft.

T.L. Das ist auch in Bezug auf eine andere Thematik interessant, zu der ich dich befragen wollte, nämlich die Topografie Singapurs und wie sie deinen kreativen Prozess beeinflusst zu haben scheint. Ich erinnere mich, wie du mir einmal sagtest, dass das Spazierengehen ein integrales Verfahren deiner Arbeit sei.

C.T. Von einem Ort zum anderen zu laufen ist natürlich Teil meines normalen Tagesablaufs, und üblicherweise suche ich für meine Spaziergänge oder Recherchen keinen speziellen Ort aus. Wenn ich bei einem Spaziergang wiederholt auf eine Vielfalt von Situationen oder Objekten treffe, dann beginne ich, über die Symbolik dieser Gegenstände und Materialien nachzudenken und wie unsere Umwelt diese Dinge hervorbringt.

In Berlin zum Beispiel findet man viele zerbrochene Glasflaschen auf der Straße, zum einen wegen der großen Verbreitung von Glasflaschen, zum anderen wegen der Trinkkultur. In Singapur entwickelt und verändert sich die Stadt fortwährend, daher findet man hier überall verteilt verschiedenste Baumaterialien: Beton, Kabel. Auch werfen die Leute hier ständig Sachen weg, überall liegen also viele Objekte herum. Aus diesen einfachen Dingen versuche ich sie zu verstehen, und dies kann mich dann zu einem umfassenderen Thema führen, das mich so sehr interessiert, dass ich weitere Nachforschungen anstelle. Ich fange also nicht mit etwas Großem an; ich beginne mit den kleinen, einfachen Dingen und verfolge rückwärts, woher sie stammen. Das ist meine Arbeitsweise.

Von einem gesellschaftlichen Standpunkt aus betrachtet, versinnbildlichen all diese Objekte auch die Gesellschaft, in der wir leben, wie wir beurteilen, was wichtig ist oder nicht, was meistens auch durch einen bestimmten Personenkreis festgelegt wird. Im Kontext Singapurs ist wichtig, dass die Bestimmung des Werts fast immer wirtschaftlichen Erwägungen folgt und kaum der historischen Bedeutung. Dies bedeutet Pragmatismus – wenn es praktischer für uns ist, ein altes Gebäude abzureißen und an seiner Stelle ein neues mitsamt der kompletten Infrastruktur aufzubauen, dann wird dies eben getan. Vielleicht erhalten wir lediglich die Fassade eines alten Gebäudes, um uns an die Vergangenheit zu erinnern, doch seinen ursprünglichen Zustand als ein zu einem bestimmten Zweck gebautes Haus wird es verloren haben.

CHUA CHYE TECK IN CONVERSATION WITH TRICIA LIM, ARTIST AND ART EDUCATOR

Tricia Lim (T.L.): Where does your photography style come from, and how did you discover it?

Chye Teck (C.T.): I was a sculptor before becoming a photographer. In order to document my sculptures after they were completed, I used photography in its most basic form to do so. The objective was to record the artworks and present them in their most literal sense, so the photography style was not fancy at all, simply a 2-dimensional reproduction of 3-dimensional originals.

When I came across objects during my daily walks, my initial instinct to photograph them also took on the same approach, i.e. using the camera as my tool to recapture the object in its purest sense. I see beauty in them, and look to these objects as individual works of art, and this is the reason I photograph them in the same manner.

The Düsseldorf School of Photography practises a very similar approach and there are definitely similarities in terms of the sense of objectivity, the respect of the original subject matter etc., but whereas the Bechers started out with an aesthetic format (structures from a specific industry, similar forms or shapes being grouped together, etc.), it was my style of recording and documenting that gave rise to the format of the multiples.

T.L. Yes, you seem to like to work in terms of serialised collecting—how do you know when to stop?

C.T. Although it first started out organically, I realised eventually and subconsciously that a collection is the best way to present a view in a photographic sense. We are able to see more clearly a view of the similarities and differences of the form of each object, and also a view of what is happening in the same place but at different times. Even if it's a tight shot, I usually include a part of the landscape in my shot. When I find that I have enough images to present a specific viewpoint, I will stop.

With *Paradise*, it took me 10 years to search for all these structures and document them. I stopped because the site I was documenting was gradually being developed into an official recreational park and the shelters simply ceased to appear. Imagine when I first came across the first one—it was so interesting that it moved me to look out for more: What are other people doing that is same or different? This kick-started my building of a collection of individual 'objects' as a collective whole idea. The subject matter is also very much in line with my on-going interest in memory and the loss or disappearance of our landscape.

T.L. This is interesting in terms of another topic I wanted to ask you about, which is on Singapore's topography and how it has seemed to inspire your creative process. I remember you once telling me that walking was an integral process of your work?

C.T. Well, walking from one place to another is part of my normal routine, and I don't normally pick a place to walk or research upon a specific area to walk. If I come across a variety of situations or objects repeatedly during a routine walk, I will start to wonder about the symbolism of these objects and materials, and how our environment produces these things.

As an example, in Berlin, you can find a lot of broken glass bottles on the streets, because of the prevalence of glass bottles and the drinking culture. In Singapore, the city is evolving and developing all the time, so we find bits of construction material strewn around: concrete, wires. Also, people here tend to throw away things fairly regularly so there are a lot of objects around. From these simple things I try to understand them, and this may lead me to a bigger topic that could interest me enough to do more research. So I don't start off with a big thing; I start with the small simple things and trace backwards to where they come from. This is how I work.

If we look at it from a social point of view, all these objects also typify the society we live in, how we judge what is or isn't important which is also usually established by a core group of people. What is important in the Singaporean context, what has value, is almost always driven by economy and not much by its historical value. This is pragmatism—if it is more practical for us to demolish an old building and build another modern one with all the infrastructure, it will be done. We may keep just a façade of an old building to remind us of the past, but it will have lost its original state as a specific purpose-built structure.

Chua Chye Teck, from the series: *Paradise (Paradies)*, photography, 2006 – 2013, each 39x35x2 cm

Chua Chye Teck, from the series: *Paradise (Paradies)*, 2006 – 2013, photography, each 39x35x2 cm

Chua Chye Teck, from the series: *Paradise (Paradies)*, 2006 – 2013, photography, each 39x35x2 cm

CHUN KAI FENG

ÜBER MEINE ARBEIT

Materielle Objekte schaffen den Hintergrund oder den Rahmen, der festlegt, wie wir uns in unserer alltäglichen Umgebung verhalten. Sie funktionieren, indem sie unsichtbar und unbemerkt bleiben, was sie üblicherweise dadurch erreichen, dass sie vertraut sind und als gegeben hingenommen werden. So grenzt etwa ein Straßengeländer den Raum ab und reguliert unsere Bewegungen in der Umwelt, doch der Gewalt, die dadurch auf uns ausgeübt wird, sind wir uns dabei niemals völlig bewusst, wir laufen in unseren täglichen Begegnungen mit ihnen vielmehr gleichgültig an ihnen vorbei.

Jedes Material hat seine eigene Zeitlichkeit. Glas ist träge und verändert sich nie. Edelstahl ist korrosionsbeständig und verfällt viel langsamer als unlegierter Stahl. Edelstahl und Glas sind Materialien, die einen Eindruck der zeitlosen Neuheit vermitteln, während rostiger unlegierter Stahl durch seine verwitterte Oberfläche das Vergehen der Zeit reflektiert.

Wenn ich aus gewöhnlichen Gegenständen Skulpturen herstelle, dann bin ich daran interessiert, einen Teil der Realität zu präsentieren und ihn zur Kontemplation in eine ästhetische Situation zu übertragen. Mein Ziel bei der Präsentation von zwei aus verschiedenen Materialien hergestellten Geländern besteht einfach darin, zu einem Vergleich einzuladen. Ich möchte die Tatsache betonen, dass jedes Material sich in einem anderen Rhythmus entwickelt und dass sich die Auswirkungen der Zeit auf sie aufgrund ihrer inhärenten Materialeigenschaften unterscheiden. Dementsprechend werden wir durch unsere Interaktion mit einem unveränderten Objekt mit einem Mal der Veränderung in uns selbst bewusst.

ABOUT MY WORK

Material objects make up the setting or frame which determines how we act in our everyday environment. They work by being invisible and unnoticed, a state they customarily achieve by being familiar and taken for granted. For example, a street railing demarcates space and regulates our movements in the environment but we are never fully conscious of the power that is exerted on us, rather we walk past them nonchalantly during our day-to-day encounters with them.

Every material has its own sense of temporality. Glass is inert and never changes. Stainless steel is corrosion resistant and deteriorates at a much slower rate than mild carbon steel. Stainless steel and glass are materials which induce a sense of timeless newness while rusted mild carbon steel reflects the passage of time through its weathered surface.

When I make sculptures of ordinary things, I am interested in putting forth a portion of reality and transplanting it for contemplation within an aesthetic situation. My purpose for presenting two railings constructed from different materials is simply to encourage a comparison. I would like to highlight the fact that every material evolves at different rhythms and the workings of time on them are different due to their inherent material properties. Correspondingly, it is through our interaction with an unchanged object that we are suddenly made aware of change in ourselves.

Chun Kai Feng, *Untitled (ohne Titel)*, 2014, stainless steel, mild steel and tempered glass (Edelstahl, Weichstahl, Hartglas), 132x132x32 cm

GERALDINE KANG

IM GESPRÄCH MIT SYLVIA POH,
IHRER MUTTER

Sylvia Poh (S.P.): Was ist das Thema deines Projekts?

Geraldine Kang (G.K.): Für mich geht es um den Tod einer Identität; ich glaube, du weißt, dass es in einer bestimmten Phase während meiner Studienzeit schwierig für mich war, zu Hause zu sein. Ich habe mit euch allen kaum ein Wort geredet und ich hatte das Gefühl, dass es für mich dort keinen Platz gab. Darum habe ich die Arbeit gemacht; es geht darum, eine Fremde in der eigenen Wohnung zu sein. Das Gleiche habe ich bei Mama (Großmutter) bemerkt, nicht dass sie dieselben Probleme gehabt hätte, aber auch sie hat mit einer Art Angst oder Depression mit sich selbst gerungen, als würde sie aus dem Kreislauf der Dinge hinausgeworfen. Ich weiß nicht, ob du das bei ihr bemerkt hast. Vor einigen Jahren gab es einen Zeitpunkt, als sie nichts mehr machen wollte und sich nur noch voller Gram ins Schlafzimmer zurückzog. Darauf basiert dieses Bild, denn das war alles, was ich von ihr gesehen habe. Ich war frustriert, dass ich ihr nicht dabei helfen konnte, sich ihren Ängsten zu stellen sowie der Tatsache, dass sie starb. Ich konnte ihr nicht ins Gesicht sagen, dass jeder den Tod durchmacht, und ich wünschte, dass sie dies nicht so schwer genommen hätte oder dass sie in der Lage gewesen wäre, mehr von sich mitzuteilen. Aber ich konnte ihr nichts vorwerfen, weil ich wusste, dass sie nicht über die Worte und über die Mentalität verfügte, dies zu tun. Die restlichen Bilder wurden nach ihrem Tod gemacht. Als junger Menschen seine Großmutter sterben zu sehen, ist erschütternd und surreal. Ich weiß nicht, wie viel Kontrolle sie darüber hatte, aber ich glaube nicht, dass es Zufall war. Es war schwer, sich mit der Tatsache abzufinden, dass ich sie nicht mehr körperlich sehen konnte. Warum betrachtest du immer das Bild von Mama im Bett?

S.P. Dieses Bild erinnert mich an die Zeit, als Mama bettlägerig war, als sie krank war, bis zu der Zeit, als sie starb. Ich bin traurig, ich denke, dass ich mehr Zeit mit ihr hätte verbringen sollen, als sie krank war.

G.K. Ist es merkwürdig, seine Mutter zu verlieren? Lässt dich das bewusster für deine eigene Sterblichkeit sein?

S.P. Ich schätze, es ist nicht besonders merkwürdig, jeder wird zu einem bestimmten Zeitpunkt den Tod erfahren; aber als sie krank war und wir über die Krebsbehandlung entscheiden mussten, nachdem sie 15 Sitzungen von Strahlentherapie hinter sich hatte, war ich mir nicht sicher, ob wir die richtige Entscheidung getroffen hatten, als wir sie zur Therapie schickten, denn nach ungefähr zehn Sitzungen war sie sehr schwach, und ich denke, sie hatte einfach nicht die Kraft zu kämpfen. Und ich glaube auch, dass ihr diese Entschlossenheit fehlte. Aber dann denke ich wiederum, dass sie wusste, dass mit ihr etwas nicht in Ordnung war, dass ihre Zeit beinahe abgelaufen war, aber im Rückblick weiß ich nicht, ob wir ihr die Wahrheit über die Diagnose hätten sagen sollen. Wie ich ihren Charakter kenne, glaube ich, dass sie der Krankheit einfach erlegen wäre. Ich bin traurig, dass sie gestorben ist, aber gleichzeitig bin ich traurig, dass ich nicht um sie weinen kann. Ich habe wohl nicht allzu viel geweint, ich konnte es einfach nicht. Die Tränen wollten einfach nicht fließen. Ich glaube, das Gleiche galt für Gong Gong (Großvater). Ich weiß nicht warum, vielleicht weil wir uns nicht so nah waren, wie ich es gerne gehabt hätte. Ich glaube, ich habe wirklich versucht, herzlicher zu sein, aber irgendwie hat es sich einfach merkwürdig angefühlt. Seit ich jung war, waren wir nicht so; wir wurden nicht so aufgezogen. Damals hat man seine Angehörigen nicht umarmt, wie es die Generation heute tut. Ich glaube, dass jeder sterben kann. Das heißt nicht, dass das Alter eine Rolle spielt. Es kann einfach jeden treffen, jederzeit. Ich glaube, jeder würde gern friedlich sterben; man hat Angst davor, leiden zu müssen, bevor man stirbt. Manche Leute leiden so viele Jahre lang, bevor sie sterben, ich glaube also, dass Mama Glück hatte, bei ihr waren es nur ein paar Monate, und ich glaube nicht, dass sie sehr gelitten hat.

GERALDINE KANG IN CONVERSATION WITH SYLVIA POH, HER MOTHER

Sylvia Poh (S.P.): What is the theme of your project?

Geraldine Kang (G.K.): To me it's about the death of an identity; I think you know that for a period of time during my university days it was very difficult for me to be at home. I wasn't really talking to all of you and I felt there was no space for me. That's why I made the work; it's about me being a stranger in my own house. I saw the same thing in Mama (Grandmother), not that she had the same issues, but that she was also struggling with a kind of anxiety or depression about herself, like she's being phased out of the cycle of things. I don't know if you picked that up from her. There came a point in time a few years ago when she didn't want to do anything and just moped about in the bedroom. This image is based on that, because that's all I saw her doing. I was frustrated about her, not being able to help her confront her own anxieties and the fact that she was dying. I couldn't say it to her face that everyone goes through death, and I wish she wasn't so difficult about it, or that she could've shared more of herself. But I couldn't blame her because I knew she did not have the words and mentality to do that.

The rest of the images were made after she died. As a young person, being the only one to see your grandmother off is very piercing and surreal. I don't know how much control she had over that, but I don't think it was coincidental. It's been hard to adjust to the fact that I no longer physically see her. Why do you keep looking at the image of Mama in the bed?

S.P. This image reminds me of the time when Mama was bedridden, when she was ill, up to the time when she passed away. I feel sad, I feel that I should have spent more time with her when she was bedridden.

G.K. Is it a strange thing to lose your mother? Does it make you more aware of your own mortality?

S.P. I guess it's not strange, everybody will experience death at a certain point but when she was ill and when we had to decide on the treatment for her cancer, after she went through the 15 sessions of radiotherapy, I wasn't sure whether we made the right decision or not, about making her go for the treatment because after about 10 sessions she was very weak, and I think she just didn't have the strength to fight. And I think also she didn't have that determination. But then again I think she knows there's something wrong with her, that her time is almost up, but looking back I don't know if we should have told her the truth about her diagnosis.

Knowing her character I think she would've just succumbed to the illness. I feel sad when she passed away, but I feel sad at the same time that I am not able to weep for her. I don't think I cried very much, I just couldn't. The tears would just not roll down. I think it was the same for Gong Gong (Grandfather), too. I don't know why, maybe it's because we weren't as close as I liked. I guess I did try to be more affectionate but somehow it just felt weird. From young we were not like that, we were not brought up that way. In those days you don't give your loved ones a hug like the generation now.

I think dying can happen to anybody, it doesn't mean that age plays a part. It can just strike anybody, anytime. I think everyone would love to die peacefully; what is frightening is having to suffer before you die. Some people suffer for so many years before they die, so I think Mama was quite lucky, it was just a couple of months and I don't think she suffered much.

Geraldine Kang, from the series: *Of Two Bedrooms (Von zwei Schlafzimmern)*, 2010 – 2015, photography, 29,7x42 cm

Geraldine Kang, from the series: *Of Two Bedrooms (Von zwei Schlafzimmern)*, 2010 – 2015, photography, 29,7x42 cm

Geraldine Kang, from the series: *Of Two Bedrooms (Von zwei Schlafzimmern)*, 2010 – 2015, photography, 29,7x42 cm

GRACE TAN & RANDY CHAN

IM GESPRÄCH MITEINANDER

Grace Tan (G.T.): Seit der Präsentation von *Building as a Body* sind drei Jahre vergangen, und du meintest, dass viele Leute, denen du begegnest, immer noch über die Arbeit sprechen. Mich würde interessieren, welche Gedanken oder Gefühle du zu dieser Arbeit hast, wenn du darauf zurückblickst, was wir gemacht haben?

Randy Chan (R.C.): Die Arbeit ist faszinierend, weil sie einen ambivalenten Status in Bezug darauf hat, was eine öffentliche Arbeit bedeutet, insbesondere wenn sie die Größe eines Gebäudes hat und temporär ist. Die Leute, die ich treffe, stellen mir Fragen, als wäre die Arbeit eine dauerhafte Fassade für diese Institution. Ebenfalls interessant ist unsere Zusammenarbeit, wie wir darüber sprechen und wie wir vorgehen. Ich schätze, darin liegt die Schönheit der Arbeit.

R.C. Besteht in deiner Arbeit ein Unterschied zwischen Maßstab und Materialität?

G.T. Mich fasziniert immer die Frage der Skalierbarkeit – wie man etwas vergrößert oder verkleinert und doch dem Wesen des Gebäudes oder des Werks treu bleibt. Bei *Building as a Body* musste die Arbeit aufgrund ihrer Größe und Beschaffenheit durch Bauarbeiter installiert werden. Zum ersten Mal wurde die eigentliche Konstruktion einer Arbeit auf andere Personen an meiner Stelle ‚übertragen', was insofern eine Abkehr von meinem üblichen Ansatz war, bei dem der Herstellungsprozess in hohem Maße intuitiv und taktil ist. Aber dadurch wurde es nicht weniger interessant, denn es war faszinierend, auf das Entstehen der Arbeit zu warten und neue Entdeckungen und Begegnungen mit ihr zuzulassen. Auch PVC war für mich etwas Neues, obwohl die Herangehensweise sich kaum davon unterscheidet, wie ich mit anderen Materialien arbeite, ihnen erlaube, die Gestaltung und die Konstruktion der Arbeit zu beeinflussen.

IN CONVERSATION WITH EACH OTHER

Grace Tan (G.T.): Three years have passed since *Building as a Body* was presented and you mentioned that people you meet still mention it. I am curious what you think or feel about the work as you look back at what we did?

Randy Chan (R.C.): The work is intriguing as it has ambivalent status in terms of the issue of what a public work means, especially when it is on the scale of a building, and temporary. People I met ask as if the work is permanently a façade to this institution which is faltering. The other interesting thing is about collaborations between us, how do we talk and get this done. I guess that is the beauty of this work.

R.C. Is there a difference between scale and materiality in your work?

G.T. I always find the question of scalability intriguing—how to scale up / scale down but yet stay true to the essence of the structure or work? For *Building as a Body*, the introduction of construction workers to install the work was required due to the scale and nature of the work. For the first time, the actual construction of a work was 'transferred' to other individuals and not myself, hence a departure from my usual approach where the making process is deeply intuitive and tactile. Nonetheless, it was not any lesser because it was enlightening to wait for the work to emerge and allow for new discoveries and encounters with the work. PVC was something new to me but the approach was pretty much the same as how I would work with other materials, allowing them to inform the design and construction of the work.

Grace Tan & Randy Chan, from the series: *Building as a Body (Gebäude als Körper)*, 2013, installation

Grace Tan & Randy Chan, from the series: *Building as a Body (Gebäude als Körper)*, 2013, installation

HO TZU NYEN

IM GESPRÄCH MIT JASON WEE

Jason Wee (J.W.): Ich möchte das Bild des Körpers in *Earth* über eine Parallele zu anderen zeitgenössischen Erscheinungsformen interpretieren, wie etwa die posthumanistische Science-Fiction, Zombiefilme wie *28 Days Later* und *Warm Bodies*, Graphic Novels wie *The Walking Dead* und *Y: The Last Man* sowie die Visionen der apokalyptischen Umweltbewegung. Sind diese Dinge für dich von Interesse?

Ho Tzu Nyen (H.T.N.): Das ist ein interessanter Ausgangspunkt, um über *Earth* zu sprechen. Ich kenne die meisten dieser Arbeiten – und sie interessieren mich durchaus. Aber wenn *Earth* tatsächlich einen Grundzug von dem aufweist, was du als apokalyptische Umweltbewegung bezeichnest, dann verdankt sich das viel eher, so glaube ich, den Filmen von Andrei Tarkowski, meinem Interesse an bestimmten Formen experimenteller Metal- und Folk-Musik und gewissen Gemälden von Caravaggio, Girodet, Gros, Géricault und Delacroix, die den menschlichen Körper in extremen Zuständen zeigen – wie etwa als penetrierten Körper, als still gestellten Körper usw. Ich schaue mir also durchaus eine ganze Menge Zombie-Filme an, würde aber sagen, dass mich dabei weniger interessiert, Zombies zu betrachten, als vielmehr, mir vorzustellen, wie ein von einem Zombie gemachter Film aussehen könnte… was möglicherweise auch eine gute Art und Weise ist, um *Earth* zu beschreiben.

J.W. Wie eine Reihe anderer Arbeiten von dir, ist *Earth* durch eine komprimierte Intertextualität gekennzeichnet, und man könnte diese Komprimierung als eine Eigenschaft des Films oder der Kunst 'in extremis' betrachten. Ich möchte noch einmal auf den Zombie zurückkommen, denn der Körper 'in extremis' ist auch die Definition des Untoten – er ist nicht ganz tot, nur scheinbar lebendig. Aber ein Zombie ist keine minimale Existenz, sondern eine exzessive Existenz, wie eine Unentschlossenheit vor der Schwelle der Sterblichkeit, auf dem Höhepunkt, bevor es in Banalität umschlägt.

In Bezug auf die Musik oder Kunst, die dir gefällt, und wenn du über neue Arbeiten nachdenkst, strebst du nach einer Art Intensität, sei es als Extrem oder als Moment des Exzesses oder der Dringlichkeit?

H.T.N. Diese komprimierte Intertextualität entspringt der Form meiner Arbeitsweise, bei der es im großen Maße darum geht, existierende Dinge, Arbeiten, Mythen neu zusammenzusetzen. Aber ich war nie daran interessiert, dass meine Referenzen verständlich sind. Für mich sind das lediglich Materialien, die nicht nur etwas bedeuten, sondern dies auf exzessive Weise tun, da sie lebendig sind. Also, ja: Ich würde sagen, dass Intensität, Energie und Exzess wichtig für mich sind, aber nur wenn sie sich endlos fortsetzen lassen und daher unendlich produktiv und fruchtbar sind, mit offenem Ende – und insofern untot. Aber als das Untote an sich, als dasjenige, was eine Potentialität besitzt und somit die Fähigkeit, zu wachsen, sich zu entfalten, so wie die höherentwickelten Zombies in Romeros *Day of the Dead*.

IN CONVERSATION WITH JASON WEE

Jason Wee (J.W.): I want to read the corporeal imagery in *Earth* alongside other parallel contemporary appearances, in post-human science fiction, in zombie cinema like *28 Days Later* and *Warm Bodies*, in graphic novels like *The Walking Dead* and *Y: The Last Man*, and also in the visions of apocalyptic environmentalism. Do any of these interest you?

Ho Tzu Nyen (H.T.N.): That's an interesting starting point for discussing *Earth*. I know most of these works - and they interest me somewhat. But if there is indeed a strain of what you call apocalyptic environmentalism in *Earth*, I think it came much more from the films of Andrei Tarkovsky, my interest in certain types of experimental metal and folk music, and certain paintings of Caravaggio, Girodet, Gros, Géricault, and Delacroix which depict the human body in extreme states—such as penetration, immobilization, etc. So I watch my fair share of zombie films, but I would say that perhaps what interests me much more than looking at zombies, is to try imagining what a film made by a zombie might look like… which might also be a good way to describe *Earth*.

J.W. *Earth*, like a number of your other works, is marked by a dense intertextuality, and it is interesting to think of its density as a feature of film or art 'in extremis'. I'm going to pick up the zombie theme again, to say that the body 'in extremis' is also the definition of the un-dead—not quite dead, only nominally alive. But a zombie isn't a minimal existence, it's an excessive one, like a hovering before mortality at its climactic edge before it ends in banality.

In the music or art you enjoy, and as you think about new work, do you pursue a kind of intensity, either as an extremity, or as a moment of excess or urgency?

H.T.N. This dense intertextuality originates in the nature of my working processes, which is a lot about re-assembling existing things, works, myths. But I've never been interested in the readability of my references. For me they are just materials that not only signify, but do so excessively, because they are alive. So yes. I would say that intensity, energy and excess are important to me but only if they can be sustained interminably, and are thus endlessly productive and generative, unbound to an end, and hence un-dead. But un-dead in itself, as that which possesses potentiality, and thus the capacity to grow, to expand, like the evolved zombies in Romero's *Day of the Dead*.

Ho Tzu Nyen, *Earth (Welt)*, 2009 – 2011, video still, 41:05 min

Ho Tzu Nyen, *The Cloud of Unknowing (Die Wolke der Unwissenheit)*, 2011, video still, 28 min

Ho Tzu Nyen, *The Cloud of Unknowing (Die Wolke der Unwissenheit)*, 2011, video still, 28 min

JEREMY SHARMA

IM GESPRÄCH MIT JOHN CHIA, SAMMLER

John Chia (J.C.): Ihre Arbeit ist eine Reflexion über Technologie. Welche Eigenschaft der Technologie versuchen Sie dabei zu erfassen? Walter Gropius etwa versuchte, die Aspekte der Entfremdung durch Technologie (in Marx' Sinne) mittels Design zu lösen usw. Welchen Aspekt oder welche Antwort auf die Technologie möchten Sie präsentieren?

Jeremy Sharma (J.S.): Ich habe nie daran gedacht, dass meine Arbeiten im engen Sinne eine Reflexion über Technologie sind. Ich habe mir darüber Gedanken gemacht, wie die Technologie gewissermaßen in die Textur unseres Lebens eingewoben und insofern unverzichtbar ist. Meiner Vorstellung von Technologie zufolge hat sie sich in den Bereich des Digitalen verschoben und kann wie ein Readymade in Kunstwerken angeeignet werden, kann neue Visionen oder Perspektiven präsentieren, kann uns neu darüber nachdenken lassen, wie wir die Malerei, Objekte oder Skulpturen betrachten. Sie unterstützt mich dabei, dorthin zu gelangen, wo ich nicht hinkommen kann, über meine physischen Grenzen hinaus. Ich bin kein allzu technischer oder wissenschaftlicher Mensch, aber ich bin an Ideen interessiert und daran, was ich in meiner Rolle als Künstler tun kann. Meine Strategie besteht außerdem darin, innerhalb des kapitalistischen Systems der aktuellen Ökonomie und des Netzwerks zu arbeiten, um in diesem Umfeld Arbeiten zu produzieren, ohne die diese Denkweise oder einfach die Art von Arbeiten, die ich produziere, nicht existieren könnten. Diese Reflexion, die Sie ansprechen, findet also statt.

J.C. Die Subspezialisierung hat für Ingenieure, Wissenschaftler, Konstrukteure von künstlicher Intelligenz, Wirtschaftsanwälte usw. völlig neue Welten geschaffen. Jedes dieser Universen ist tief und ansonsten (für den Außenseiter) undurchdringlich. Wie kann ein Künstler die Kluft überwinden – und alle diese Welten kommentieren, nicht nur die Welten, die er kennt?

J.S. Genau deswegen gefällt mir das, aber ich arbeite zu meinen eigenen Bedingungen. Diese Bedingungen definieren die Kunst, die produziert wird, und setzen einen Rahmen, auf den ich mich stützen kann. Diese Universen sind in der Tat undurchdringlich, und es ist die Rolle des Künstlers, diese Welten miteinander zu verbinden, damit sie für den Betrachter zugänglich sind. Dadurch werden diese Dinge nicht unbedingt leichter verständlich, und noch viel weniger werden irgendwelche Probleme gelöst. Ihre Fragen gehen in eine Richtung, auf die meine Praxis hinsteuert, es ist also durchaus eine Vision, mit der ich mich beschäftige. Ich glaube, letztlich läuft es auf das menschliche Moment hinaus, weshalb wir Kunst machen, und es hängt weniger mit hintergründigen, als vielmehr sehr einfachen Vorstellungen zusammen. Meine neueren Arbeiten und Versuche handeln in Wirklichkeit vielleicht davon, wie wir Objekte wahrnehmen oder wie wir Landschaften betrachten, aber dies lässt sich mit künstlicher Intelligenz verbinden oder mit dem Übernatürlichen oder sogar mit der Appropriation. Die Materialität zieht den Mythos nach sich sowie eine Form der Transformation des Kunstwerks. In letzter Zeit hat mich die Frage des Betrachters als Konsument interessiert, wie er in unserer heutigen Welt tatsächlich auftritt, während der Künstler diese Art von Sinneserfahrung oder Begegnung mit dem Betrachter schafft, sei es durch ein Objekt, sei es durch einen Raum. Aber ich beabsichtige dies durch Systeme, Programme oder Daten zu verwirklichen. Damit ist also der Rahmen oder das Konzept gegeben, und dann versuche ich, Spezialisten auf diesem Gebiet zu finden, da mir die Fachkenntnis und die technische Kompetenz fehlen. Und durch diese Spezialisierungen, wie Sie sie genannt haben, konnten viele Spezialisten ihr Expertenwissen an jemanden wie mich weitergeben, wodurch dann ein Netzwerk oder ein gemeinsames Bewusstsein geschaffen wird.

J.C. Glauben Sie, dass zeitgenössische singapurische Künstler abgesehen von traditionellen asiatischen Formen und Kontexten der globalen/westlichen Kunst und Kultur irgendetwas Besonderes hinzufügen haben?

J.S. Das kann ich wirklich nicht beantworten. Ich vermute, mit Blick auf Singapur würde man sich fragen, warum dieses winzige Land überhaupt so sehr an zeitgenössischer Kunst interessiert ist und warum es diese Art von Künstler hervorbringt. Die Verknüpfung des Westlichen mit dem Globalen mag problematisch erscheinen, und der Kontext ist letztlich mit dem Ort verbunden. Meine Arbeit könnte als von traditionellen asiatischen Formen und Kontexten am weitesten entfernt angesehen und vielmehr in Bezug zur westlichen Kunstgeschichte verstanden werden, doch vielleicht äußert sie sich in der traditionellsten Form, die sich darauf bezieht, woher ich stamme.

JEREMY SHARMA IN CONVERSATION
WITH JOHN CHIA, COLLECTOR

John Chia (J.C.): Your work tries to reflect technology. What quality of technology are you trying to capture? E.g., Walter Gropius was trying to solve the alienating aspects of technology à la Marx through design etc. What aspect or response to technology do you represent?

Jeremy Sharma (J.S.): I have never thought, in a strict sense, of reflecting technology in my works. I have thought about how technology is sort of embedded in the fabric of our lives and is indispensable in that sense. My notion of technology now is that it has moved into the realm of the digital and that it is readymade and can be appropriated into artworks, present new visions or vistas, rethink how we look at painting, objects or sculpture. It assists where I can't go, beyond my physical limitations. I'm not the most technical or scientific person but I am interested in ideas and what I can do in my position as an artist. My strategy is also to work within the capitalist system of the present economy and network to make works within that environment, outside of which this mode of thinking or simply the kinds of works I'm producing could not exist. So there is that reflection that you are talking about.

J.C. Sub-specialization has created whole new worlds for engineers, scientists, computer artificial intelligence designers, corporate lawyers, etc. Each of these universes is deep and otherwise impenetrable (to the outsider). How can an artist cross the gap—and comment on any world—other than the one he knows?

J.S. That's exactly why I like it but I do it on my own terms. Those terms define the art being produced and give me a framework to base upon. These universes are rightly so, impenetrable, and it's the role of the artist to bridge these worlds together for the viewer to absorb. It doesn't necessarily make these things easier to understand,

and even less so, solve any problems. Your questions are framed in the way that my practice is veering towards, so it is a vision I am invested in. I think in the end, it ultimately comes down to the human element of why we make art, and it's tied down to very simple ideas, not really profound ones. My recent works and forays could really be about how we perceive objects or how we look at landscapes, but you can connect that to artificial intelligence, or the supernatural or even appropriation. With materiality comes myth and some sort of transformation of the artwork. I have recently been interested in the idea of the viewer as a consumer, which is true in our present world, and the artist creating that sort of sense experience or encounter with the viewer; it could be an object, it could be a room. But I think about materialising this through systems, programme or data. So that forms the framework or the concept, then I start looking for specialists in that area because the subject knowledge and technical expertise is beyond me. And these specializations, as you call it, have led many specialists to farm out their expertise to someone like me, and then this network or shared consciousness is created.

J.C. Outside the vernacular of Asian forms and context, do you think Singapore contemporary artists have anything special to add to global/western art culture?

J.S. I really don't know. I guess if you are looking to Singapore, you would be wondering what makes this tiny country so interested in contemporary art in the first place and the kinds of artists it is producing. Linking Western to global may seem problematic and context in the end is tied to location. My work could be seen as the least vernacular of Asian forms and context and could be framed in terms of Western art history, but may in fact speak in the most vernacular of forms relating to where I come from.

Jeremy Sharma, *Mode Change* (gallery view installation) *(Modus-Wechsel)* (Galerieansicht der Installation), 2014, Polystyrene EPS foam, cast polyurethane foam with pigment (Styropor EPS-Schaum, gegossener Polyurethan-Schaum mit Pigmenten), dimensions variable (unterschiedliche Größen)

Jeremy Sharma, *Unicorn (Einhorn)*, 2014, EPS foam, PU paste and duratec with white pigment (EPS-Schaum, PU-Paste und Duratec mit weißen Pigmenten), 2 parts 96×215×81,5 cm, 2 parts 136×160×42 cm

Jeremy Sharma, *As-is-where-is (butts and ends)*, 2014, Polystyrene EPS foam (EPS-Polystyrolschaum), dimensions variable (unterschiedliche Größen)

TAN PIN PIN

DREI FRAGEN, DIE ICH MIR SELBST GESTELLT HABE:

I. Was wolltest du mit diesem Film erreichen?

Ich wollte die Verbindung zwischen Bild, Text und dem gesprochenen Wort ausweiten.

II. Was ist das absolute Minimum, um im Kino eine narrative Erfahrung zu schaffen?

Ich vermute, dass es keinen Unterschied macht, ob die Bilder an den Erzählorten gefilmt wurden oder nicht und ob die erzählten Ereignisse wirkliche Ereignisse waren. Aber sie wurden an den realen Orten gefilmt, und diese Ereignisse haben tatsächlich stattgefunden. Das Reale scheint immer mein Ausgangspunkt zu sein. Diese Verbindung ist für den Film wichtig.

III. Wie wichtig ist Struktur?

Für das Projekt haben wir die Kamera fest arretiert und die Menschen vom Set entfernt. Im Rückblick hätte ich in einem geeigneten Moment mit dieser selbstauferlegten Regel brechen können, um über diese Struktur selbst zu kommentieren.

THREE   QUESTIONS   I
ASKED   MYSELF:

[I.] What were you trying to achieve with this film?

I wanted to stretch the connection between image, text and the spoken word.

[II.] What is the barest minimum needed to create a narrative experience in the cinema?

I suppose that it did not matter whether the images were filmed in the locations narrated or not, or whether the events narrated were actual events. But they were filmed in the actual locations, and these events did take place. The realm of the real always seems to be my starting point. It is important for the film to have that connection.

[III.] How important is structure?

In the design of the project, we locked the camera still and removed people from the set. In retrospect, I could have broken this rule I had set for myself at an opportune moment, to comment on the structure itself.

Tan Pin Pin, *The Impossibility of Knowing (Die Unmöglichkeit des Wissens)*, 2010, video still, 11:31 min

Tan Pin Pin, *To Singapore, With Love (In Liebe zu Singapur)*, 2013, video still, 2:01 min

VINCE ONG

IM GESPRÄCH MIT KELVIN ANG, DIREKTOR DES AMTS FÜR DENKMALSCHUTZ DER URBAN REDEVELOPMENT AUTHORITY (URA)

Kelvin Ang (K.A.): Ich weiß, dass du dich von den ästhetischen Idealen des ‚Gesamtkunstwerks' inspirieren lässt. Könntest du erläutern, wie du diese Philosophie in deinen Arbeiten einsetzt?

Vince Ong (V.O.): Die Vision, einen in sich zusammenhängenden Raum zu schaffen, indem man die verschiedenen ‚Gewerke' der Handwerkskunst vereint, ist nicht neu. In der Renaissance gab es keine strikte Trennung zwischen Architektur, Innenarchitektur, Skulptur, Malerei und sogar dem Ingenieurswesen. Frank Lloyd Wright arbeitete mit Künstlern und Handwerkern zusammen, um Gebäude, Innenräume und Objekte zu schaffen, die in ihrer allgemeinen Form, den Details und den Oberflächen miteinander harmonieren. In einem ‚Gesamtkunstwerk' wird berücksichtigt, wie die Objekte innerhalb eines architektonischen Raums platziert sind; um diese physischen Beziehungen herzustellen, arbeite ich mit Handwerkern aus verschiedenen Bereichen zusammen. So besteht *Calla von Voch* etwa aus handgefertigten Lichtobjekten, die durch eine von Metallhandwerkern und Stuckateuren gemeinsam konstruierte physische Basis visuell mit der Decke verbunden sind. Die durch diese Basis geschaffene visuelle Kontinuität lenkt den Blick des Betrachters von den Objekten zur Decke und weiter auf den übrigen Raum, wodurch sie als Ganzes verstanden werden können, während zugleich vor unserem ‚geistigen Auge' die Vorstellung einer Komplexität entsteht. Bei dieser Vorgehensweise werden die Grenzen verwischt, und jedes Mal, wenn ich an einem neuen Projekt arbeite, versuche ich diese Technik zu verfeinern.

K.A. Diese ‚Vorstellung einer Komplexität' scheint ein wiederkehrendes Thema deiner Arbeiten zu sein. Könntest du das näher erläutern?

V.O. Als Designer suche ich nach Schönheit in den Dingen und Räumen, die ich schaffe. Schöne Objekte oder Räume sind in der Lage, einen Blick festzuhalten, die Augen von einer Ecke des Raumes zur anderen zu leiten, sei es durch eine formale Narration oder durch die Komposition. Zum Beispiel ist der gopuram (Eingangsturm) des Sri-Mariamman-Tempels (Singapurs ältester Hindu-Tempel) deshalb schön, weil er dem Blick Halt gewähren kann, ebenso wie die Wieskirche in Bayern. Die skulpturalen Stuckarbeiten und Freskomalereien in dieser Kirche leiten den Blick von der zweidimensionalen Repräsentation zur dreidimensionalen Form, die sich gegenseitig einrahmen, wodurch die Erfahrung des architektonischen Raumes beeinflusst wird. Einen ähnlichen Sinn für Schönheit möchte ich mit meinen Designarbeiten erreichen.

K.A. Mit dem, was du erreichen willst, scheint ein großes Maß an fachkundiger Handarbeit und Maßfertigung verbunden zu sein, was in einem Umfeld, in dem vorrangig auf Effizienz und eine oberflächlich verstandene ‚Produktivität' Wert gelegt wird, ein Luxus ist. Wie siehst du dies in Singapur oder auch in Asien realisiert, wo die traditionellen Handwerksberufe schnell verschwinden?

V.O. Wir sollten nicht der Illusion erliegen, dass Sachen schnell und gut gemacht werden können. Gute Dinge brauchen ihre Zeit, um hergestellt zu werden. Beim Fertigungsprozess geht es nicht nur um gute Verarbeitung, sondern er ist auch ein Mittel für die Handwerker, um ihren Kreationen eine ‚Seele' einzuhauchen; und daher brauchen gute Dinge ihre Weile. Wir sollten unser Augenmerk darauf richten, wie wir die Produktionszeit verkürzen können, ohne dabei jedoch Kompromisse in Bezug auf die Möglichkeit der Maßfertigung einzugehen. Meiner Meinung nach müssen wir Technologie in den Handwerksprozess einführen, um Individualisierung und Variation in der Massenproduktion zu erlauben und um eine neue Generation von Handwerkern hervorzubringen, die in der Lage sind, andere Werkzeuge wie etwa 3-D-Drucker, 3-D-Software usw. zu verwenden. Auf diese Innovation arbeite ich hin, ihre Materialisierung sehe ich in meinen Designarbeiten.

VINCE ONG IN CONVERSATION WITH KELVIN ANG, DIRECTOR OF CONSERVATION MANAGEMENT, URBAN REDEVELOPMENT AUTHORITY (URA)

Kelvin Ang (K.A.): I understand that you draw inspiration from the aesthetic ideals of 'Gesamtkunstwerk' ('Total Work of Art'). Can you explain how you apply this philosophy in your creations?

Vince Ong (V.O.): The vision to create a cohesive space by marrying the different 'trades' of Crafts and Arts isn't new. The Renaissance saw no strict division between architecture, interior design, sculpture, painting and even engineering; Frank Lloyd Wright worked with artists and craftsmen to create buildings, interior spaces and objects that resonate with each other in their overall form, detailing and finishes. A 'Total Work of Design' is the consideration of how objects sit within an architectural space; I work with craftsmen from different trades to create these physical relationships. For instance, *Calla* by *Voch* consists of handcrafted lighting objects connected visually to the ceiling by a physical base which was built by metal and plaster craftsmen working together. The visual continuity, created by the base, leads the gaze of a person from the objects to the ceiling and onwards to the rest of the space, allowing a person to read them as a whole while at the same time triggering the notion of intricacy in our 'Mind's eye'. It's an approach that blurs boundaries, a technique which I strive to hone each time I work on a new project.

K.A. This 'notion of intricacy' seems to be a recurring theme in your works. Can you elaborate on that?

V.O. As a designer, I seek beauty in the things and spaces I create. Beautiful objects or spaces are able of holding one's gaze, of leading one's eyes from one end of the room to another, either through a narrative of forms or composition. For example, the gopuram (entrance tower) of Sri Mariamman Temple (Singapore's oldest Hindu temple) is beautiful because of its ability to hold one's gaze, as with the cathedral of Die Wieskirche in Bavaria, Germany. The sculptural stucco works and frescoes painting in the cathedral lead one's gaze from two-dimensional representation to three-dimensional form, framing each other, affecting the experience of the architectural space. And I wish to achieve a similar sense of beauty in the design works I create.

K.A. What you aim to achieve seems to involve quite a bit of skillful craft and customization, which is a luxury in an environment that prioritizes efficiency and a superficial understanding of 'productivity'. How do you see that being implemented in Singapore, or even in Asia, where traditional craft trades are fast disappearing?

V.O. We shouldn't have the illusion that things can be made fast and good. Good things take time to be created. The process of crafting isn't just about good workmanship but it is also a means by which craftsmen imbue 'soul' into their creations, and hence good things last a long time. We should focus on how to shorten the production time but without compromising on the ability to customize. I see the introduction of technology into the process of crafting as the way ahead, to allow for customization and variation in the process of mass production and to create a new generation of craftsmen who are able to use a different set of crafting tools such as 3-D printers, 3-D mapping software, etc. This novelty is something that I am working on and I see it materializing in my own design works.

Vince Ong, *TABLE #2 (Tisch #2)*, 2015 , stainless steel, polished (rostfreier Stahl, poliert), 285 x 90 x 210 cm

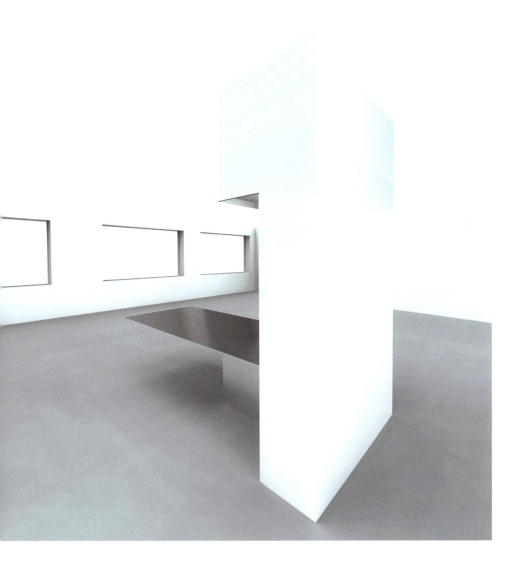

ZAI TANG

IM GESPRÄCH MIT JOLEEN LOH,
KURATORIN UND SCHRIFTSTELLERIN

Joleen Loh (J.L.): *Respect (Bukit Brown Cemetery I)* bringt gleichzeitig zwei verschiedene Arten und Weisen, Abstraktion zu ‚lesen', zum Ausdruck: die Nichtwahrnehmbarkeit von Klang, (der mit den Polaritäten von Abstraktion und Konkretion, Denken und Körper, Privatem und Öffentlichem niemals ganz zufrieden ist), und die amorphen Formen, die die visuelle Notation be-/entvölkern. Worin besteht für dich bei der Beschäftigung mit dem Sozialen und Politischen der Reiz des Nichtrepräsentativen?

Zai Tang (Z.T.): Abstraktion ist für mich ein Verfahren, das nach einer Wahrheit jenseits der Erscheinungen sucht. Die Notation zu dieser Arbeit ist eine Übersetzung der immanenten Eigenschaften der Klänge, die mir in Bukit Brown begegneten, in die visuelle Form. Sie verdeutlicht einen Teil des Wesens dieser Klänge, das ansonsten schwer zu fassen ist.

Ich habe die Notation geschaffen, während ich meine Außenaufnahmen anhörte und dabei von jeder visuellen Assoziation mit der Quelle absah, die sie hervorgebracht hat, sei es ein Vogel, ein Säugetier, eine Amphibie oder ein Insekt. Sobald diese Klänge entkörperlicht werden, offenbaren sie ihr Innenleben; ihre gestischen, klangfarblichen und zeitlichen Transformationen treten in den Vordergrund.

Bei dem Versuch, die verborgenen Ausdrucksweisen der Lebewesen kenntlich zu machen, die ich auf dem Friedhof Bukit Brown gehört hatte, habe ich, glaube ich, sowohl sie selbst als auch den Ort, den sie bevölkern, näher kennengelernt. Doch in Anbetracht der Tatsache, dass durch diesen Friedhof eine Autobahn gebaut wird, sprechen diese Klänge nun mit einer gewissen Fragilität zu mir; ihre verschwindende Präsenz ist eine Form des stillen Protests gegen die gnadenlose Maschinerie des Kapitalismus – doch wer hört wirklich zu?
Wenn wir offene Ohren haben, können wir unser Bewusstsein mit größerer Klarheit

auf das richten, was um uns herum geschieht. Mit meiner Arbeit hoffe ich zu dieser Aufmerksamkeit anzuregen. Die Abstraktion ist nur ein Mittel zu diesem Zweck.

J.L. Klang ist dem Körper stets gleichzeitig innerlich wie äußerlich. Seine emotionale Ansteckungsfähigkeit mobilisiert unsere innere Welt und öffnet uns auf unsere Umgebung hin. Lässt sich deine Arbeit als Wunsch nach Intimität mit der Öffentlichkeit verstehen, mit dem Anderen, dem Nicht-Menschlichen und dem Nicht-Vertrauten?

Z.T. Ich sehe meine Arbeit als den Prozess, die Poetik des Klangs im Verhältnis zum Sein zu verstehen; als Versuch, das Zuhören als ein Mittel zu erweisen, um eine tiefere Verbindung mit unserer unmittelbaren Erfahrung der Welt einzugehen.

Mich interessiert, wie Klanglandschaften unsere Erfahrung des Ortes beeinflussen, insbesondere in städtischen Umgebungen, wo anthropogene (vom Menschen gemachte) Klänge oftmals über diejenigen der Natur dominieren. Ich glaube, dieses Ungleichgewicht trägt zu einem stärkeren Gefühl der Entfernung von dem anderen Leben bei, mit dem wir unsere Heimat teilen; inmitten der Klanglandschaften der Moderne werden unsere Ohren zunehmend taub, wodurch es für uns immer schwerer wird, die leiseren, peripheren Klänge zu vernehmen, mit denen wir gemeinsam existieren.

In einer Zeit, in der unser herrschendes Wirtschaftsmodell im extremsten Widerspruch zu unserer Umwelt funktioniert, ist es entscheidend, dass wir unsere Beziehung zur Natur überdenken und eine neue Verbindung mit ihr eingehen, nicht nur als ein von uns getrenntes Objekt, sondern auch als etwas, mit dem unsere Existenz verbunden ist. Und hier kommt das Zuhören ins Spiel.

Sei für einen Moment ruhig. Was hörst du?

ZAI TANG IN CONVERSATION WITH JOLEEN LOH, CURATOR AND WRITER

Joleen Loh (J.L.): *Respect (Bukit Brown Cemetery I)* embodies two different modes of 'reading' abstraction simultaneously: the imperceptibility of sound (which is never quite content with the polarities, between abstraction and concretion, thought and body, private and public) and the amorphous forms that (dis-)inhabit the visual score. What is the lure of the non-representational for you in engaging with the social and political?

Zai Tang (Z.T.): For me, abstraction is a process that searches for truth beyond appearances. The score for this work is a translation of the intrinsic characteristics of the sounds I encountered at Bukit Brown into visual form. It exposes part of their essence that is otherwise elusive.

I created the score whilst listening to the dubplate of my field recordings, ignoring any visual associations to the source that created them, whether bird, mammal, amphibian or insect. These sounds, once disembodied, reveal their inner life; their gestural, timbrel and temporal transformations come to the fore.

In attempting to uncover the hidden expressions of the creatures I heard at Bukit Brown, I feel I have come closer to knowing them and the place they inhabit. However, in the light of the highway that is being constructed through the cemetery, these sounds now speak to me with a certain fragility; their fading presence a form of quiet protest against the unrelenting machinery of capitalism—but who is really listening?

With our ears engaged we can attune our consciousness to what is happening around us with greater clarity. It is this awareness that I hope to stimulate within the people who encounter my work. Abstraction is just a means to that end.

J.L. Sound is always interior and exterior to the body. Its affective contagiousness mobilizes our inner world and opens us up towards our surroundings. Can we speak of your work as a desire for intimacy with the wider public, to the other, the non-human and the unfamiliar?

Z.T. I see my work as a process of understanding the poetics of sound in relation to being; an attempt to expose listening as a means of forming a deeper connection to our immediate experience of the world.

I'm interested in how soundscapes affect our experience of place, particularly in urban environments where anthropogenic (or human-made) sounds often dominate those of nature. I believe this imbalance contributes to a greater sense of dislocation from the other life we share home with; our ears are becoming increasingly numb amidst the soundscape of modernity, making it harder for us to hear the quieter, peripheral sounds with which we co-exist.

At a time when our dominant economic model functions at extreme odds to our ecology, it is vital that we reassess how we relate to nature, reconnecting with it not as an object separate from ourselves, but as something that our very existence is tethered to. This is where listening comes into play.

Be still for a moment. What do you hear?

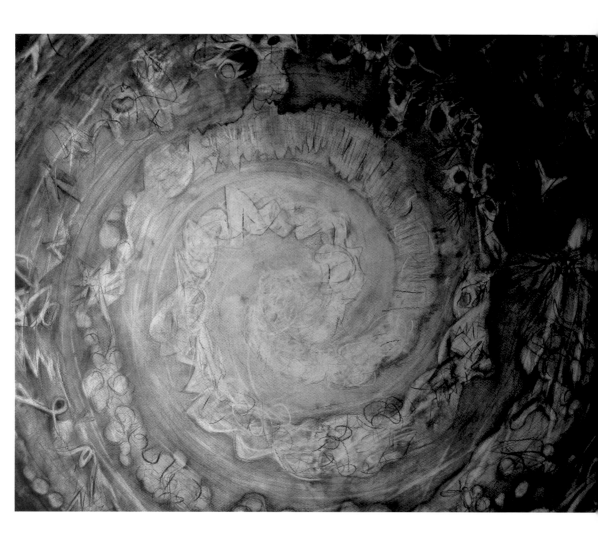

Zai Tang, *Respect III (Bukit Brown Cemetery I) (Respekt III [Friedhof Bukit Brown])*, 2015, graphite, ink, charcoal and digital print (Graphit, Tinte, Kohle, Digitaldruck), 70x70 cm

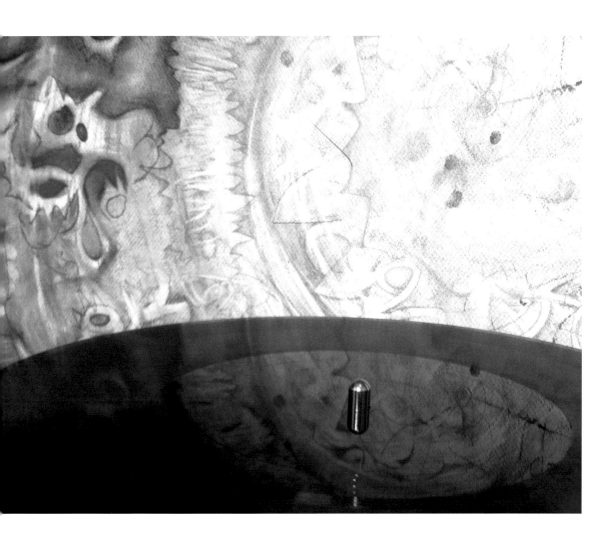

ENCOMPASS

ANCA RUJOIU
"WE ARE ALL FOREIGNERS"

WHAT THE MODERN
NATION-STATES FAIL
OFTEN TO ACKNOWLEDGE
IN   AND
THEIR CLASSIFICATION
SYSTEMS IS THAT
WE DO BELONG
TO MANY PLACES

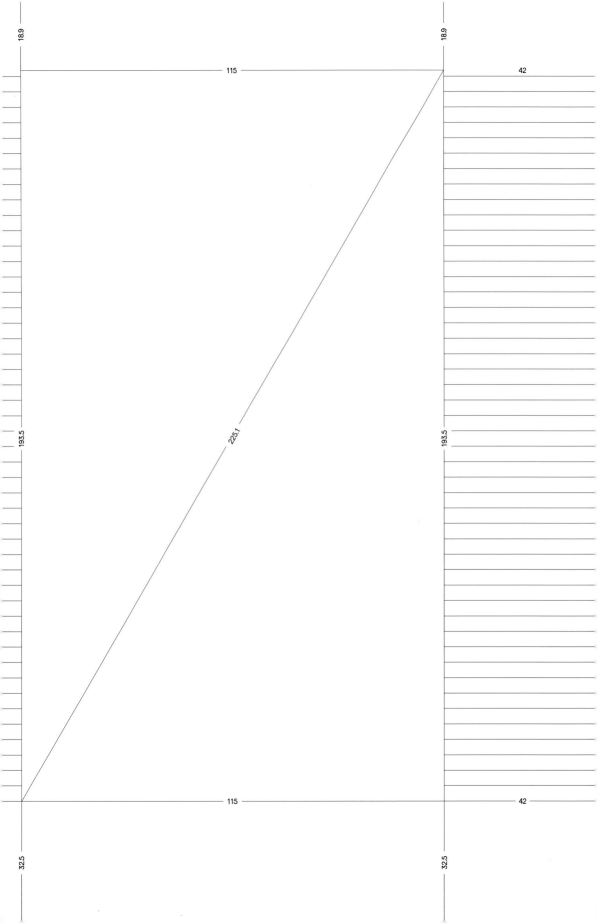

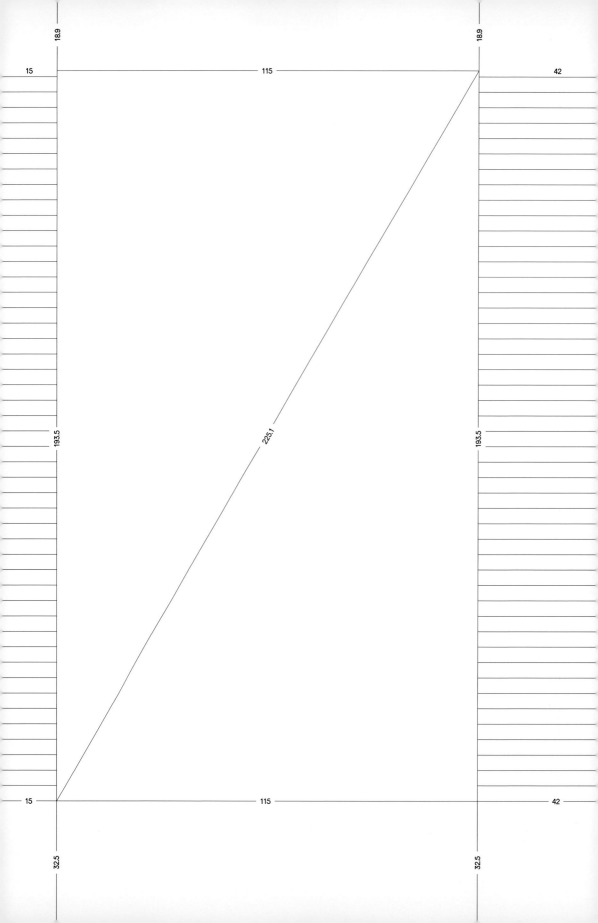

WIEDER NEU MACHEN
Michael Lee

Derzeit beschäftige ich mich abwechselnd damit, diesen Essay zu schreiben und die Renovierungsarbeiten in dem Haus zu überwachen, das ich vor kurzem gekauft habe und das auch als mein Atelier fungieren wird. Während ich mich mit dem Staub und den Wartezeiten herumplage und zusammen mit der Baufirma penibel alle Mängel behebe, habe ich mir die Frage gestellt, ob das Hausbesitzerdasein die renovierte Version meiner vormaligen hypothekenfreien Existenz ist. Etwas zu ‚renovieren' heißt es ‚wieder neu machen' – abgeleitet von den lateinischen Etyma ‚re' (wieder) und ‚novare' (neu machen). Auch wenn es mir immer gefallen hat, über meinen eigenen Bereich zu verfügen, ohne durch ein Bankdarlehen belastet zu sein, war dieses alte, freigeistige und mietezahlende Selbst für mich kaum noch reizvoll. Es war Zeit für eine Erneuerung – wieder einmal.

Ruhelosigkeit liegt mir im Blut. Mein Vater wurde kurz nach seiner Geburt in Teluk Anson (heute Teluk Intan) im malaysischen Bundesstaat Perak verkauft. Als Teenager auf der Suche nach Chancen, wanderte er nach Singapur aus, wo er meiner Mutter begegnete. Ich wurde 1972 geboren und lebte 26 Jahre lang mit meiner permanent umziehenden Familie in nicht weniger als neun verschiedenen Wohnungen in allen Teilen Singapurs. Als mit schwankenden finanziellen Situationen vertraute Geschäftsleute gingen meine Eltern keinerlei Wetten auf Beständigkeit oder Dauerhaftigkeit ein – schon gar nicht, was die Wohnung betraf. Verbesserungen, Renovierungen oder Verschlechterungen waren unbestrittene Normalität, ebenso wie die Scheidung. Noch heute bin ich ihnen dafür dankbar, dass sie ihre Ehe an einem gewissen Punkt für beendet erklärten. Damit setzten sie ein Beispiel für die Möglichkeit, sich auf eine Situation oder einen Ort einzulassen und ihn dann, wenn die Zeit abgelaufen ist, wieder zu verlassen.

Eines meiner neun Elternhäuser war eine Dreizimmereckwohnung im elften Stock eines HDB-Plattenbaus[1] an der Depot Road. Hier wohnte ich am längsten, von 1979 bis 1989. Hier kämpfte ich mit Langeweile. Mehr als einmal dachte ich daran, aus dem Fenster zu springen – aber nicht, weil ich dieses Lebens oder dieser Wohnung überdrüssig gewesen wäre. Vielmehr wollte ich auf sehr handfeste Weise prüfen, ob dieses Leben real war und was jenseits von ihm geschehen könnte. Offenkundig – und zum Glück – bin ich nicht dazu gekommen, mich mit diesen existenziellen Fragen zu beschäftigen, denn ziemlich bald wurden Fenstergitter angebracht.

Also wandte ich mich wissenschaftlichen Experimenten zu, die ich von der Schule nach Hause brachte. Ich züchtete Bohnensprossen und baute diverse Objekte, unter anderem ein Haus aus Papier und Zucker, in dem Ameisen gedeihen konnten. Ich besaß auch ein Aquarium, das laufend vervollkommnet wurde. Mein Interesse wandte sich immer wieder neuen Spezies zu. Dann, eines Tages, in der Hektik des Zusammenpackens vor dem Umzug, entsorgte mein Vater die aquatische Fauna in der Toilettenschüssel.

Unserem Elternhaus entflohen wir in ein anderes Zuhause: eine Fünfzimmerwohnung am Boon Lay Drive. Zweimal im Jahr, sobald die Schulferien begonnen hatten, fuhren mein ältester Bruder und ich für jeweils einen Monat in die Wohnung meiner Pateneltern. Einige ihrer verheirateten Kinder – unsere Patengeschwister – versammelten sich dort mit ihren eigenen Kindern zum Abendessen. Danach wurde die Wohnung für vielfältige Nutzungen umgeräumt. Während der Festtage wurden Extratische

---

1. Das Housing and Development Board (HDB) wurde 1960 als staatliches Verwaltungsorgan für den sozialen Wohnungsbau in Singapur gegründet.

ausgeklappt, um Platz für Spiele zu bieten, und die Erwachsenen stellten beim Mahjong ihr Glück und ihr Können auf die Probe. Mit jeder Umgestaltung der Einrichtung wurde die Wohnung meiner Patin neu gemacht. Vielleicht ist dies der Grund dafür, weshalb ich es nachfühlen kann, wenn Dinge nur in der beschränkten Weise benutzt werden, für die sie vorgesehen sind, und somit Gelegenheiten verpasst werden.

Auch wenn ich die Regeln des Mahjong lernte und einige Runden spielte, hat mich das Spiel selbst sehr viel weniger fasziniert als seine Elemente. Während der Spielpausen eilte ich stets zu dem Tisch mit den zeitweise sich selbst überlassenen, ‚Ziegeln' genannten Mahjong-Spielsteinen. Beinahe so viel Spaß wie das Aufstapeln der *Ziegel* zu Strukturen in allen Formen und Größen machte es mir – zum Entsetzen der Erwachsenen – sie umzustoßen. Dieses selbsterfundene Spiel spiegelte die Umgebung wieder, in der ich aufwuchs: Stadtentwicklung und -erneuerung in verkleinertem Maßstab und in schneller Aufeinanderfolge. Mein anhaltendes künstlerisches Interesse für den Raum, die Struktur und das Modellbauen führe ich auf diese kindlichen Streiche zurück.

Die Wohnung meiner Mutter in der Sin Ming Avenue war die letzte Wohnung, in der ich lebte, bevor ich auszog. Meine Mutter kaufte die nicht mehr ganz neue Dreizimmerwohnung, als sie bereits geschieden war. Während sie eines der Schlafzimmer ihren Kindern zuwies, hatten ihre Arbeitsmaterialien alle anderen Bereiche der Wohnung eingenommen. Sie arbeitete – und arbeitet noch heute – in der Gastronomie. Wir hatten mehrere Garnituren von allem und jedem: Stapel von Gewürzpackungen und Türme aus Geschirr. Diese Konstruktionen waren wie Altäre: Man durfte sie nicht bewegen und schon gar nicht mit ihnen herumspielen. Die Wohnung war unser Schlafsaal und für meine Mutter ein Vorratslager. Meine jüngere Schwester zog als Erste aus. Sie heiratete und siedelte in die Vereinigten Staaten um. Ich zog aus, als meine damalige Lebensgefährtin mir von einer freien Wohnung erzählte. Bald darauf packte auch mein jüngster Bruder seine Sachen, ohne sich richtig zu verabschieden. Verständlicherweise war meine Mutter nicht begeistert.

Auszuziehen bedeutet seine Unabhängigkeit auf räumliche Weise geltend zu machen. Ich war des Lebens im ‚Schlafsaal' überdrüssig und hatte während eines Jahres Arbeit genügend Geld angespart – in ungefähr derselben Zeit, die ich mit meiner damaligen Freundin zusammen war. Ich war entschlossen, unser ‚Liebesnest' an der Bedok South Road zu einem behaglichen Ort zu machen. Diese Dreizimmer-HDB-Wohnung der neuen Generation, die wir mit einer Kollegin meiner Freundin teilten, war mit ihren Originalkacheln und der Ausstattung aus den 1980er Jahren bescheiden, und wir richteten sie sparsam ein. Ich bemühte mich sehr darum, alles sauber und reinlich zu halten, bis hin zum Einsatz von Pinzetten, um Schmutz in schwer zugänglichen Ecken zu entfernen. Aber das sollte sich schon bald darauf ändern.

Schnell überwucherte meine wachsende Sammlung von Büchern, Notizen und Manuskripten aus der Recherche für meine Abschlussarbeit alle Räume. Das Chaos war notwendiger Teil meiner Arbeit, aber ich vermute, es war auch eine unbewusste Methode, um einen nicht mehr willkommenen Gast zu vertreiben: meine Lebensgefährtin. Fest entschlossen, den robusten Kommunikationsstil meiner Eltern nicht zu wiederholen – zu den markantesten Zeichen zählten Löcher in den Türen und zerbrochene Möbelstücke, – bildete ich eine passive Aggression aus, die sich räumlich manifestierte: im Mangel an guter Haushaltsführung.

Vielleicht wurde das Projekt *Stud House* (2003), ein Modell unseres idealen Zuhauses (oder meiner Vorstellung unseres idealen Zuhauses), das ich meiner Freundin zum Geschenk machte, zu einer Art Wiedergutmachung. *Stud House* beschäftigte sich mit einer autobiografischen Frage: Wie können zwei Menschen zusammenleben, ohne einander überdrüssig zu werden? Diese sorgenvolle Frage wurde in einer aufreibenden Phase sondiert, als sich in unserer Beziehung bereits Überdruss und Routine eingestellt hatten. Ich wählte des Modalverb ‚können' statt des einfachen Indikativs ‚leben', weil ich die Hoffnung auf Optionen hegte und weil ich nicht realisierte, dass die Neugier und die Möglichkeit, die in den Worten ‚wie können' enthalten sind, die Rhetorik der Unmöglichkeit des Satzes von Anfang an Lügen strafen.

Wir renovieren, weil wir einen Neustart wollen, alles umkrempeln wollen. Fünf Monate nach der Trennung endete der Mietvertrag für die Wohnung. Ich beschloss, das Angebot meiner Schwester anzunehmen, ihre Fünfzimmerwohnung in der Simei Road zu mieten, während sie sich in den USA einrichtete. Die Renovierung dieser Wohnung rettete mich vor dem Stillstand: vor der Last und der Bedrängnis des bestehenden Lebens in all seinen Formen. Aber letzten Endes ist das Renovieren ein utopischer Akt: Es strebt nach einem trügerischen Paradies, enthält lediglich ein teilweise leeres Versprechen auf eine bessere Welt. Dinge und Geschmäcker nutzen sich ab und verwandeln sich mit der Zeit. Und dann wird bald wieder Zeit für eine weitere Renovierung sein.

Ich glaube nicht, dass ich mich bei meinen Mitbewohnern in der Simei Road jemals dafür werde ausreichend entschuldigen können, dass ich ein so schlechter Mitbewohner war. Oft mussten sie auf Zehenspitzen im Haus herumlaufen, um nicht auf meine Materialien, Werkzeuge oder halbfertigen Kunstwerke zu treten. Für sie war dies eine Art aufgezwungener Renovierung, denn ich hatte unser gemeinsames Wohnzimmer in mein Privatatelier umgestaltet. Sie verdienen einen Preis für Toleranz und dafür, dass sie beide Augen zudrückten sowohl gegenüber dem Chaos, das ich veranstaltete, als auch der hohen moralischen Ebene, auf die ich mich stellte, als ich versuchte, das Haus in eine „Wohnmaschine" zu verwandeln. Dieser Begriff von Le Corbusier stellte das traditionelle Haus infrage, indem er es als einen Ort der Produktivität und der Effizienz postulierte. Douglas Darden revidiert Le Corbusier, wenn er behauptet, dass „ein Haus zum Sterben da ist."[2] Und überhaupt, wie sehr unterscheiden sich Leben und Sterben? Meine neuere Neonarbeit *Machine for ~~Living~~ Dying In* (2013) reflektiert über dieses Paradox.

Teilweise ergab sich das ‚Scheitern' meiner Wohnungen in Bedok und Simei aus der Verschmelzung von Arbeit und Wohnen und von Häuslichkeit und künstlerischer Produktion in Wohngemeinschaftssituationen. Bebauungsvorschriften bestehen nicht ohne Grund: Bestimmte Formen der Arbeit können gefährlich sein, wenn sie in einem Wohnzimmer ausgeführt werden. Dennoch hielt ich an meinem Wunsch fest, das ideale Wohnatelier zu finden. Ich war enthusiastisch, als ich gegen Ende meiner viermonatigen Zeit als Gastdozent an der Universität Hongkong eine Wohnung zur Miete fand, die im Viertel Fo Tan in den Neuen Territorien gelegen war. Hier wurden die Bebauungsvorschriften locker interpretiert. Die Studio Bibliothèque, ein experimenteller Arbeitsraum, entstand, indem ich den Gewerbebetrieb mit all meinen Habseligkeiten füllte, hauptsächlich meiner Büchersammlung aus Singapur.

Ich musste die Halle kaum renovieren; sie besaß bereits den Stil, den ich haben wollte. Diese 90m² große Halle im Wah Luen Industrial Centre hatte einen schönen Zementstrichboden und eine von den Vormietern eingebaute Galerie. Ich unterstrich den kalten, industriellen Eindruck, indem ich den Fußboden mit Zinkplatten auslegte, wie sie in alten Bussen verwendet wurden. Diese Entscheidung sollte ich später bereuen, als der Winter anbrach. Der Akt des Renovierens hat viel mit Identität zu

---

2. Douglas Darden, *Condemned Building*, New York: Princeton Architectural Press, 1993.

tun. Insbesondere hoffen wir, dass der neu gemachte physische Raum unsere innere Welt – unsere Persönlichkeit, unseren Geschmack und unsere Hoffnungen – widerspiegelt oder, besser noch, bereichert. Nicht nur einmal war ich von der Tatsache überwältigt, dass ich mich nun einen anerkannten Künstler nennen konnte, einfach deshalb, weil ich ein richtiges Atelier besaß. Atelier und Künstler sollten fortan unzertrennlich wie siamesische Zwillinge sein.

Einen Monat, bevor der zweijährige Mietvertrag auslief, war ich bereit – sowohl das Atelier wie die Stadt – zu verlassen. Davor war ich blind gegenüber den weniger zuträglichen Aspekten der Räumlichkeiten, darunter das Fett und der Rauch aus den Barbecue-Läden im selben Stockwerk. Früher fand ich es reizvoll, nach Hongkong und wieder zurück zu reisen. Zwei Jahre später stellte sich die Furcht ein, in das Verhörzimmer geführt zu werden, wo mich ein Grenzbeamter aus Hongkong wegen meiner häufigen Reisen befragen würde. Außerdem hatte ich, nachdem ich bei der Guangzhou Triennale (2008) Singapur und Hongkong ‚vertrat', den Eindruck, so weit gekommen zu sein, wie ein Künstler dort kommen könnte. Und was am wichtigsten war, mir war das Geld ausgegangen. Doch der befreundete Künstler Leung Chi Wo hat wahrscheinlich den wahren Grund erfasst: „Du hast es nicht geschafft, in Hongkong Liebe zu finden", meinte er.

Die Gründe dafür, mein Atelier in Hongkong aufzugeben, unterscheiden sich nicht allzu sehr von denen, mein Berliner Atelier aufzugeben. Berlin war ein Aha-Erlebnis. Während meines einjährigen Aufenthaltsstipendiums im Künstlerhaus Bethanien traf ich viele Künstler, sah zahlreiche ausgezeichnete Ausstellungen und habe gute Freunde gewonnen. Ich verlängerte meinen Aufenthalt, indem ich ein Zimmer mietete, das eines von zwei Ateliers sein sollte. Zwei Standbeine zu haben, schien für einen singapurischen Künstler in der Mitte seiner Karriere eine berufliche Notwendigkeit zu sein. Wir singapurische Künstler stammen aus einem kleinen Teil der Welt und sind wohl auf größere Aufmerksamkeit angewiesen. Doch vier Monate nach Unterzeichnung des Mietvertrags realisierte ich, dass ich das nicht mehr wollte. Nicht nur war es finanziell aufreibend, in zwei Städten die Miete aufzubringen, sondern ich war es auch überdrüssig, ein Leben mit Beziehungspflege aufrechtzuerhalten, wie es von Künstlern in Berlin generell erwartet wird. Inzwischen hatte ich auch ein neues Interesse gefunden: eine HDB-Wohnung in Singapur zu besitzen.

Ich bin also wieder da, wo ich angefangen habe. Wird dieses Atelier der Rückzugsort sein, den ich immer gesucht habe? Oder wird es neue Ängste beherbergen? Es ist für mich nicht mehr abzusehen, ob es das eine oder das andere sein wird. Ich denke darüber nach, warum ich Künstler geworden war, über die Bestimmung des Künstlers, Neues zu machen, wieder und wieder. Die meiste Zeit meines Lebens hatte ich das Neumachen unwissentlich in Räumen praktiziert, die sowohl Rückzugsorte wie Schlachtfelder waren, vielleicht ist es also müßig, über das Versprechen oder das Paradies zu grübeln, das im Renovieren stecken könnte. Nur das Machen ist von Bedeutung.

MAKING NEW, AGAIN
Michael Lee

At the moment, I switch between writing this essay and supervising the renovation of my recently bought home, which will also serve as my studio. As I deal with the dust and waiting, and meticulously rectify errors with the contractor, I begin to wonder if being a homeowner is the renovated version of my previous mortgage-free existence. To 'renovate' is 'to make new, again'—derived from the Latin etyma 're' (again) and 'novare' (make new). Though I have always enjoyed being in my own space without the burden of a bank loan, this old self, free-spirited and rent-paying, was hardly sexy to me anymore. It was time for a renewal—again.

Restlessness is in my blood. My father was sold soon after he was born in Telok Anson (now Telok Intan) in the state of Perak, Malaysia. As a teenager in search of opportunities, he wandered into Singapore, where he met my mother. I was born in 1972, and for 26 years after that I lived with my serial-moving family in no fewer than nine different homes across Singapore. As businesspersons familiar with volatile financial situations, my parents never placed any bets on permanence or stability in business—much less in the area of home. Upgrading, renovating and downgrading were unquestioned norms, and so was divorce. I am still grateful to them for calling their marriage quits at some point. They set examples for the possibility of entering a situation or place, and then leaving when the time is up.

Among my nine family homes was a three-room corner unit on the eleventh floor of an HDB[1] slab block on Depot Road. I lived there for the longest period of time, from 1979 to 1989. Here, I wrestled with boredom. More than once I thought of jumping out of the window, not because I had had enough of this life or this flat. Rather, I wanted to examine, in a very tangible way, if this life was real and what could happen beyond it. Obviously and thankfully, I did not get to address these existential questions, for window grilles were soon installed.

So I turned to science experiments brought home from school. I grew bean sprouts and built things, including a paper sugar house in which ants could thrive. I also had an aquarium that was endlessly updated. My interest in specific species kept changing. Then, one day, in his haste to pack up and move, my father disposed of the aquarium life into the toilet bowl.

Escape from our family home was to another home: a five-room flat on Boon Lay Drive. Twice a year and lasting a month each time, my eldest brother and I made our way to my godparents' home as soon as the school holidays started. A few of their married children—our god-siblings—would gather there with their kids for dinner. In the evenings, the flat was transformed for a variety of uses. During festive holidays, stored tables were unfolded to provide room for games, and groups of adults pitted their luck and skills against one another in mahjong. Godma's flat was made new each time the furnishing was reconfigured. Perhaps this is why I sympathise with the missed opportunities of things used only in the limited ways that they are built for.

Though I learned the mahjong rules and played a few rounds, the game proper did not excite me as much as its parts. During breaks in the game, I would rush to the table of temporarily abandoned mahjong tiles. Almost as fun as stacking the tiles into structures of all shapes and sizes was knocking them down, much to the adults' dismay. This self-invented game reflected the environment I grew up in: urban development

---

1. HDB, which stands for Housing and Development Board, was established in 1960 as the statutory board responsible for public housing in Singapore.

and renewal on a reduced scale and in quick succession. I trace my ongoing artistic interest in space, structure and model making to this childhood escapade.

Mum's flat on Sin Ming Ave was the last apartment I stayed in before moving out. She bought the resale three-room flat as a divorcee. While she apportioned one of the bedrooms to her kids, her work stuff had taken over all other parts of the apartment. She was—and still is—in the F&B (food and beverage) industry. We had multiple sets of everything: piles of packaged seasoning and towers of crockery. These structures were like altars: they were not to be moved, not to mention be fooled around with. The flat was our dormitory, and Mum's storage space. My younger sister was the first to vacate. She got married and moved to the States. I left when my then partner informed me of a flat available for rent. Soon after, my youngest brother also packed up without bidding a proper goodbye. Understandably, Mum was not thrilled.

Moving out is an assertion, in spatial terms, of independence. I had enough of 'dormitory' living and had saved enough from a year of working, about the same duration since having met my then partner. I was determined to make our 'love nest' at Bedok South Road cosy. This three-room New Generation HDB flat we shared with my partner's colleague was humble with original 1980s tiles and fittings, and we furnished it simply. I took pains to keep things clean and neat, to the extent of using pincers to remove dirt from tight corners. But that was just at the beginning.

Quickly, the space started to clutter with my growing collection of books, notes and manuscripts from the research for my graduate thesis. The mess was a necessary part of my work, but I suspect it was also an unconscious way to evict a no-longer-welcome guest: my partner. Having resolved not to repeat my parents' assertive communication—holes in the door and broken furniture were among the prominent signs—I developed a passive aggression that manifested spatially: in the lack of good housekeeping.

Perhaps the 2003 project *Stud House*, a model of our ideal home (or my idea of our ideal home) made as a gift to my partner, became a kind of atonement. *Stud House* addressed an autobiographical question: How can two persons live together without getting sick of each other? The question, steeped in anxiety, was explored during a stressful period when fatigue and familiarity had established themselves in the relationship. I chose the auxiliary verb 'can' instead of 'do', hoping for options, and not realising that, from the onset, the curiosity and possibility in 'how can' belie the phrase's rhetoric of impossibility.

Renovation takes place because we want a fresh start, inside out. Five months after the breakup, the lease for the flat expired. I decided to accept my sister's invitation to rent her five-room Simei Road home while she took up residence in the States. Renovating this flat saved me from stasis: from the weight and oppression of existing life in all its forms. But renovating is ultimately a utopian act: it aspires towards an elusive paradise, holds only a partially empty promise of a better world. Things and tastes wear, tear and change over time. And then, soon, it will be time for another renovation again.

I don't think I can ever apologise enough to my fellow tenants in Simei for being a bad flatmate. They often had to tiptoe around the house to avoid stepping on my materials, tools or artworks-in-progress. For them, this was a kind of imposed renovation, for I had refashioned our shared living room into my own private studio. They ought to be given awards for tolerance and for turning a blind eye to both the mess I made and the moral high ground I stood on, where I tried to make the house 'a machine for living in'. This Corbusian phrase challenged the conventional home by embracing it as a site for productivity and efficiency. Douglas Darden revises Corbusier, suggesting that 'a house is for dying'.[2] Indeed, how different is living from dying? My recent neon light piece, *Machine for ~~Living~~ Dying In* (2013), reflects on this paradox.

In part, the 'failures' of my Bedok and Simei flats were due to the conflation of work and home, and domesticity and artistic production, in co-sharing situations. Zoning regulations have reasons for existing: the nature of certain types of work can be hazardous if set in a residential space. Still, I persisted in searching for the ideal home studio. I was ecstatic when, towards the tail end of my four-month stint as a visiting lecturer at a university in Hong Kong, I found a unit up for rent in Fo Tan, located within the New Territories. Here, zoning regulations were loosely interpreted. *Studio Bibliothèque*, an experimental work space, was born from filling the industrial unit with all my belongings, mostly my book collection from Singapore.

I did not need to renovate the unit much; it had the style I wanted. This 90m^2 unit within the Wah Luen Industrial Centre had a beautiful cement screed floor and an in-built loft left by the previous tenant. I further emphasised the cold, industrial feel by using zinc panels for the loft's flooring, the way they were used in old buses. It was a decision I regretted slightly when winter came. Renovating has much to do with identity. We especially hope that the renewed physical space reflects our inner world—our personality, tastes and aspirations—or better still, enhances it. More than once I felt overwhelmed with the fact that I could now pronounce myself an accomplished artist, simply because I had a proper studio. Studio and artist would henceforth be inseparable like conjoined twins.

With a month to go before the two-year lease was up, I was ready to leave—both the studio and the city. I had been blind to the less attractive aspects of the space, including the grease and fumes from the barbecue businesses occupying the same floor. I used to find travelling in and out of Hong Kong charming. Two years later, I began to fear being led into the interrogation room, where a Hong Kong immigration officer would question my frequent movements. Also, having 'represented' Singapore and Hong Kong at the 2008 Guangzhou Triennial, I felt I had gone as far as I could as an artist based there. Most importantly, I had run out of money. But my artist-friend Leung Chi Wo probably got the real reason right: "You didn't manage to find love in Hong Kong", he said.

The reasons for closing my Hong Kong studio are not too different from that of my Berlin studio. Berlin was an eye-opener. During my one-year residency programme in Künstlerhaus Bethanien, I met many artists, saw numerous good shows and made good friends. I extended my stay by renting a bedroom, which I wanted as one of two studios. Having two bases seemed a professional necessity for a Singaporean mid-career artist. We Singaporean artists come from a small part of the world, and, arguably, require greater exposure. But four months after taking up the lease, I realised I did not want it anymore. Not only was it financially draining to sustain rent in two cities, there was also weariness from maintaining the networking life expected of any artist in Berlin. By then, I had also found a new interest: owning an HDB flat in Singapore.

So I am back to where I began. Will this home studio be the sanctuary I have always sought? Or will it habour fresh anxieties? I can no longer foresee whether it will be one or the other. I think about why I became an artist, about the artist's calling to be making new, again and again. For most of my life, I had unknowingly practised making new in spaces that were both sanctuaries and battlegrounds, so it is perhaps futile to ponder about the promise or paradise that renovating could yield. Only the making matters.

2. Douglas Darden, *Condemned Building*, New York: Princeton Architectural Press, 1993

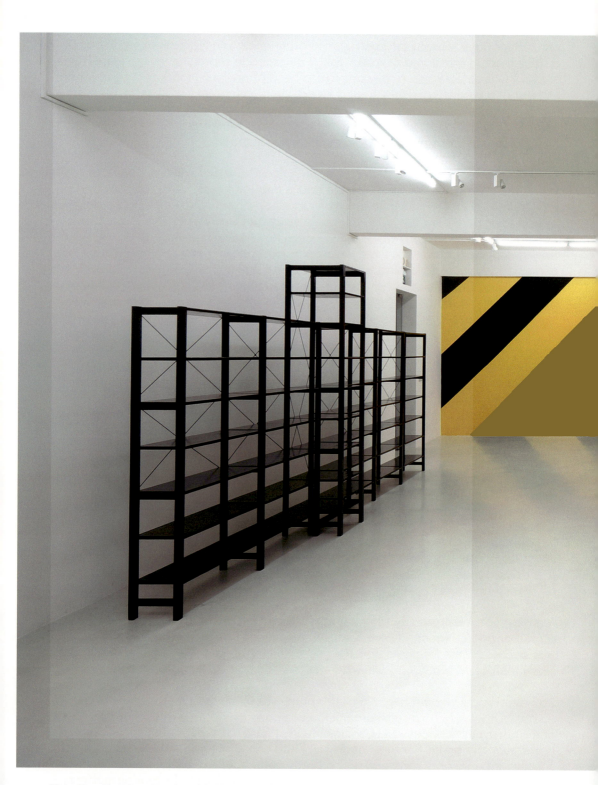

Michael Lee, *Script for an Unperformed Performance No. 1 (Skript einer nicht aufgeführten Aufführung Nr.1)*, 2014, found hammock and vinyl text (gefundene Hängematte und Vinyltext), dimensions variable (unterschiedliche Größen) from the exhibition, *Machine for ~~Living~~ Dying In (Maschine, um darin zu ~~leben~~ sterben)*, 2014

DAS SINGAPORE ART ARCHIVE PROJECT: VON YISHUN IN DIE GILLMAN BARRACKS
Koh Nguang How

Anfänge

Das *Singapore Art Archive Project (SAAP)*[1] ist ein fortlaufendes Projekt (eine ortsspezifische Installation), das ich 1999 begonnen habe, als ich an eine HDB-Dreizimmerwohnung[2] in Yishun New Town gelangte, nachdem ich seit 1983 mit meinen Eltern in einer Vierzimmerwohnung im selben Block gelebt hatte. Diese privaten Räume sollten meine wachsende Sammlung von Materialien zur Kunst und Kultur in Singapur und anderen Ländern, die ich seit 1980 besuchte, beherbergen. Mit dem Sammeln der Materialien in meiner eigenen Wohnung konnte ich auch den Aufenthalt von ausländischen Künstlern und Wissenschaftlern ermöglichen. Immer häufiger stellte ich die Materialien für die Forschung und für Projekte von Besuchern aus Singapur und dem Ausland zur Verfügung. Es gestaltete sich jedoch immer schwieriger, diese umfassenden Materialien in meinen kleinen, vor allem auf Wohnbedürfnisse zugeschnittenen Räumlichkeiten zugänglich zu machen.

Im Jahr 1999 existierte in Singapur lediglich das National Archive, das 1968 gegründet worden war und dessen Aufgabe in der Aufbewahrung von Dokumenten mit nationaler und historischer Bedeutung bestand, wozu kaum Künstler und Kunstereignisse zählten. Die Gründung des *Asia Art Archive*[3] in Hongkong im Jahr 2000 inspirierte mich dazu, an einer besseren Lösung für mein eigenes Archivprojekt zu arbeiten, für das meine winzige Wohnung nicht mehr ausreichte.

Sammlung und Fotografie

Meine Sammlung für das *Singapore Art Archive Project* begann mit Zeitungsausschnitten (auf Englisch und Chinesisch) für Studienzwecke, als ich 1980 die Oberstufe besuchte. Ich belegte unter anderem das Fach Kunst, also richtete sich meine Aufmerksamkeit natürlich vorwiegend auf Artikel über Kunst. Noch heute sammle ich Zeitungsausschnitte.

Meine erste Anstellung hatte ich von Oktober 1985 bis Januar 1992 als Museumsassistent in der National Museum Art Gallery (NMAG)[4] in Singapur. Zu meinen Aufgaben als Mitarbeiter des Assistenz- und des Chefkurators zählten die Katalogisierung, die Lagerung und das Auffinden von Objekten. Dieses Umfeld ermöglichte es mir, Künstler, Kuratoren und andere Persönlichkeiten aus der Kunstwelt zu treffen und mit ihnen zu arbeiten. Die NMAG war ein bekannter und zentraler Ort, an dem lokale Künstler und Künstlergruppen ausstellten; es gab eine große Bandbreite an Veranstaltungen wie etwa Ausstellungen, Vorträge, Workshops und Wettbewerbe. So wuchsen allmählich meine Erfahrungen mit Kunst und verwandten Themen ebenso wie meine Sammlung entsprechender Materialien.

Die Fotografie gehörte zwar nicht zu meinen Aufgaben in der NMAG, aber sie war ein wesentliches Moment bei der Erfassung von Objekten sowie der Vorbereitung

---

1. Der Name *Singapore Art Archive Project* wurde erst 2005 eingeführt.
2. Das 1960 gegründete Housing und Development Board (HDB) ist die staatliche Verwaltung des öffentlichen Wohnungsbauprogramms Singapurs. Heute leben über 80% der Singapurer in HDB-Wohnungen, während es im Jahr der Gründung des HDB nur 9% waren.
3. Das *Asia Art Archive* wurde im Jahr 2000 in Hongkong als Reaktion auf das dringende Bedürfnis gegründet, die vielfältige jüngere Geschichte des zeitgenössischen Kunst in der Region zu dokumentieren und zu sichern. Diese Sammlung enthält heute über 50.000 Dokumente, die aus mehreren hunderttausend physischen und digitalen Elementen bestehen, und wird fortlaufend erweitert.
4. Die National Museum Art Gallery (NMAG) wurde 1976 als Teil des (seit 1887 bestehenden) National Museum mit öffentlichen und privaten Geldern gegründet, um moderne Ausstellungsräumlichkeiten und einen Mehrzweck-Theatersaal zu bieten. Mit der Gründung des Singapore Art Museum 1993 wurde sie geschlossen.

von Ausstellungen; ich eignete mir Grundkenntnisse an und begann bei Veranstaltungen wie Ausstellungen, Eröffnungsfeierlichkeiten, Pressekonferenzen, Vorträgen, Workshops und Atelierbesuchen Fotos zu machen. Im Juni 1987 erhielt ich von meinem Kurator meinen ersten offiziellen Auftrag als Fotograf bei dem vom Ministerium für Stadtentwicklung (Ministry of Community Development, MCD) und dem National Museum ausgerichteten fünften ASEAN-Jugend-Malerei-Workshop.[5] Dort konnte ich die Arbeitsmethoden verschiedener anerkannter Maler und junger Kunststudenten aus den sechs Staaten Südostasiens beobachten. Im August begann ich meine erste ernsthafte Fotodokumentation über Performancekunst: eine viertägige Performance-Veranstaltung von Tang Da Wu[6] mit dem Titel *Four Days at National Museum Art Gallery*. Während meiner Tätigkeit im Museum erweiterte sich meine Sammlung um neue Materialien: Einladungskarten für Ausstellungen, Kataloge, Poster, Flyer, Fotografien, Videos und Tonaufnahmen. Wenn ich nicht bei Kunstveranstaltungen war, fotografierte ich außerdem die physischen Veränderungen der ländlichen und städtischen Gegenden in Singapur. Mich interessierten die verschwindenden Landschaften rund um mein neues Zuhause (eine HDB-Wohnung); nachdem ich das dörfliche Umfeld meiner Kindheit verlassen hatte, versuchte ich, die Erinnerungen durch Fotografie wiederzugewinnen. Als die Dörfer später verschwunden waren, fotografierte ich Stadtszenen in der Nähe des National Museums, in dem ich arbeitete.

Koordination und Forschungsaufträge

Anfang 1992 verließ ich die National Museum Art Gallery, um mich ausschließlich meiner Arbeit als Künstler zu widmen und trat der neu registrierten Künstlergruppe The Artists Village[7] bei. Gelegentlich reiste ich als Künstler und sammelte an den Orten, die ich besuchte, Materialien für das *SAAP*.

Im Jahr 1996 ergab sich für mich die Gelegenheit, für das Fukuoka Art Museum in Japan die Koordination des Ausstellungsprojekt *The Birth of Modern Art in South East Asia: Artists and Movements* zu übernehmen. Durch meine Beteiligung an dem Projekt erfuhr ich mehr über einige ältere und vergessene Künstler, über deren Werke sowie über die frühe Geschichte der Kunst Singapurs. Nach dem Ende dieses Projekts im Fukuoka-Museum beschloss ich, mein Hauptaugenmerk auf die Dokumentation der schnell verschwindenden Arbeiten und Erfahrungen älterer Künstler zu richten. An diese älteren Materialien gelangte ich durch diese Künstler selbst ebenso wie über Flohmärkte, Antiquariate, Buchverkäufe, leerstehende Gebäude und Mülldeponien.

Vom neu gegründeten Fukuoka Asian Art Museum in Japan erhielt ich im Rahmen des neuen Researcher/Curator in Residence-Programms ein Aufenthaltsstipendium von September 1999 bis Februar 2000. Dieser Aufenthalt führte zu einer ernsthafteren Beschäftigung mit dem Sammeln und der Forschung über die frühen Generationen von Künstlern und künstlerischen Aktivitäten in Singapur, auch der vergessenen. Damit wuchs die Menge an Materialien über die ältere Kunstgeschichte von Singapur weiter an; über die Möglichkeiten der Digitalisierung und Erhaltung dieser

---

5. Die Association of Southeast Asian Nations (ASEAN) wurde am 8. August 1967 in Bangkok von Indonesien, Malaysia, den Philippinen, Singapur und Thailand gegründet. Die ASEAN hatte das Ziel, Frieden und Stabilität in der Region zu fördern und der Ausbreitung des Kommunismus in den Staaten Südostasiens Einhalt zu gebieten. Brunei Darussalam trat am 8. Januar 1984 bei, Vietnam am 28. Juli 1995, Laos und Myanmar am 23. Juli 1997 und Kambodscha am 30. April 1999. Der fünfte ASEAN-Jugend-Malerei-Workshop (einschließlich einer Ausstellung) fand 1987 in Singapur statt und wurde gemeinsam vom Ministerium für Stadtentwicklung und dem Singapore National Museum ausgerichtet. Der erste ASEAN-Jugend-Malerei-Workshop wurde 1983 in Bangkok abgehalten. Das letzte und sechste Gastgeberland für die Reihe von Workshops war 1988 Brunei.
6. Tang Da Wu ist ein bedeutender zeitgenössischer Künstler aus Singapur; 1985 erhielt er seinen MA Fine Art am Goldsmiths College, University of London. Seit seiner Rückkehr nach Singapur im Jahr 1988 beschäftigt er sich mit Performancekunst.
7. The Artists Village wurde 1988 in einem Bauernhof im Norden Singapurs als erste Künstlerkolonie für junge zeitgenössische Künstler gegründet. Das Gelände wurde 1990 von der Regierung für die militärische Nutzung erworben. 1992 registrierten die verbliebenen Künstler ihre Gruppe offiziell als The Artists Village (TAV). Die Gruppe setzt ihre Aktivitäten derzeit ohne feste Räumlichkeiten fort, unter anderem organisiert sie ein Residenzprogramm auf der Insel Pulau Ubin in der Nähe des internationalen Flughafens Changi.

Materialien machte ich mir ernsthafte Sorgen. Inzwischen hatte ich eingesehen, dass es mir unmöglich war, zwei verschiedene Stränge – den der zeitgenössischen und den der vergangenen Kunstgeschichte – gleichzeitig zu dokumentieren und zu erforschen. Also beschloss ich, weniger Zeit und Mittel für jüngere Künstler und zukünftige Ereignisse aufzuwenden, insbesondere seit dem Aufkommen des Internets und digitaler Aufnahmegeräte in Singapur. Somit entstand eine Sammlung von beinahe 300 Fotorollen mit Ereignissen aus der Kunst und dem Leben von 2002 bis 2003, die bis heute nicht entwickelt worden sind. Was aufgrund mangelnder finanzieller Möglichkeiten, die Bilder zu entwickeln und abzuziehen, als eine Ansammlung von Filmen begann, wurde dann zu einer Arbeit, die sich mit verlorenen Erinnerungen, verlorenen Archiven und dem Verzicht der Dokumentation zukünftiger Ereignisse beschäftigte.

Archive als Inhalt und Medium der Kunst

Im Jahr 2004 war ich für eine Einzelausstellung von der neuen kuratorischen Initiative p-10 eingeladen, die in der Nähe von Little India in Singapur beheimatet ist, wo eine Reihe junger Künstler ihre Wohnungen in Ateliers umwandelte. Ich wollte der neuen Künstlergemeinschaft einige meiner Archivmaterialien präsentieren, und daraus entstand die von p-10 kuratierte Ausstellung *Errata: Page 71, Plate 47. Image Caption. Change Year: 1950 to Year: 1959; Reported September 2004* by Koh Nguang How. Kurz gesagt, basierte die ERRATA-Ausstellung auf der falschen Datierung eines Gemäldes des Künstlers Chua Mia Tee, das die Einführung des Malaysischen als Nationalsprache des neuen souveränen Staates Singapur zum Thema hatte, in dem Buch *Channels & Confluences. A History of Singapore Art* (1996) von Kwok Kian Chow, dem Direktor des Singapore Art Museum (SAM). Ich präsentierte mehrere Gruppen älterer Publikationen aus meiner Sammlung, um dem Publikum Hinweise und Auskünfte für die korrekte Datierung des Gemäldes zu geben. Das Publikum konnte dabei einige seltene Veröffentlichungen betrachten und durchblättern. Die *Errata*-Ausstellung wurde 2005 darüber hinaus an zwei weiteren Orten präsentiert: in der NUS Central Library, gemeinsam von p-10 und dem University Scholars Programme organisiert, sowie im Singapore History Museum. Die Ausstellung beinhaltete eine Reihe von Arbeiten, bei denen ich Archivmaterial präsentierte, das das Publikum sowohl als archivalische Quelle als auch als Material für ein installatives Kunstwerk ansehen konnte.

Nachdem die Ausstellung *Errata* positiv aufgenommen worden war, erhielt ich 2005 ein Aufenthaltsstipendium von *p-10*. Hier verwendete ich erstmals den Namen *Singapore Art Archive Project* (SAAP); das SAAP@p-10 sollte eine Quelle von Archivmaterial zur zeitgenössischen Kunst in Singapur sein, für die die bestehenden Materialien meiner Sammlung genutzt wurden. Es sollte der Recherche über die zeitgenössische Kunst in Asien und deren Netzwerke dienen. Dieses Projekt behandelte auch Fragen der Aufbewahrung, der Datenerfassung und grundlegender Archivpraktiken und lief von Januar bis Juli 2005. Nach meinem Aufenthalt bei p-10 wurde von Juni bis August 2005 in der Ausstellung *Situation: Collaborations, Collectives and Artist Networks from Sydney, Singapore and Berlin* im Museum of Contemporary Art in Sydney die Vernetzung singapurischer Künstler thematisiert. Ich präsentierte eine Zeitleiste und Archivmaterialien zur Gruppe The Artists Village. 2008 war ich mit meinem Archiv auch bei der Ausstellung *The Artists Village: 20 Years On* im Singapore Art Museum beteiligt.

Im Jahr 2011 wurde ich eingeladen, eine Arbeit für *Open House* – die 3. Singapore Biennale bei 8Q im Singapore Art Museum (8Q-SAM) – zu produzieren. Ich nutzte die Gelegenheit, um meine im Laufe von dreißig Jahren gesammelten Zeitungsausschnitte ebenso wie zahlreiche vollständige Ausgaben zu zeigen. Die Installationsarbeit trug den Titel *Artists in the News* (auch SAAP@8Q-SAM), und bestand aus englischen und chinesischen Morgenzeitungen vor allem aus den Jahren 1980 bis 2011. Die Zeitungen wurden in verschiedenen Themenblöcken auf Wänden, die wie große Pinnwände funktionierten, sowie in kleineren Installationsarbeiten präsentiert. Ich hob insbesondere einen Artikel über die ‚wegbereitende' Installation von Tang Da Wu vom April 1980 mit dem Titel *Earthworks* heraus, um auf die dreißig Jahre später stattfindenden künstlerischen Entwicklungen in Singapur und der Welt zu verweisen. 1980 wurden diese *Earthworks* allerdings von dem damaligen Direktor des National Museum vorzeitig beendet. Ironischerweise wurde auch die Mixed-Media-Installation *Welcome to the Hotel Munber* des japanisch-britischen Künstlers Simon Fujiwara auf derselben Biennale vom Singapore Art Museum zensiert.

2013 wurde die Gründung des NTU Centre for Contemporary Art, Singapore (CCA)[8] in dem neuen Kunstzentrum der Gillman Barracks bekanntgegeben. Es folgte eine Einladung an mich für ein Aufenthaltsstipendium in den Gillman Barracks, das von Juli 2014 bis Januar 2015 lief. Dort präsentierte ich das *Singapore Art Archive Project@CCA* (*SAAP@CCA*), während im CCA gleichzeitig die Ausstellung *No Country: Contemporary Art for South and Southeast Asia* stattfand, in der auch der singapurische Künstler Tang Da Wu vertreten war, dessen künstlerische Performances einen wesentlichen Bestandteil in meinem Archiv zeitgenössischer Kunst ausmachten. Die Sammlung für das *SAAP@CCA* ist die bislang umfangreichste; sie umfasst Zeitungen, Einladungskarten, Flyer, Kataloge, Zeitschriften, Poster, Dia- und Negativfilme, Fotografien, Tonaufnahmen und Kunstwerke. Das *SAAP@CCA* sollte auch die Recherche und die Zusammenarbeit zwischen den verschiedenen eingeladenen Künstlern, Kuratoren des CCA und Gastkuratoren sowie Wissenschaftlern ermöglichen.

Zukunft des Singapore Art Archive Project

Mit dem Ende meines Aufenthalts am 31. Januar 2015 ist das *SAAP@CCA* abgeschlossen; diese Archive, die bis auf die 1920er Jahre zurückgehen, sind dann in meine Wohnung und die meiner Eltern in Yishun zurückgekehrt. Sie harren auf ihren nächsten Gastgeber oder ihr Schicksal.

---

8. Das NTU Centre for Contemporary Art Singapore ist ein Forschungszentrum der Technischen Universität Nanyang, das vom Economic Development Board Singapurs gefördert wird. Es ist neben einer Reihe internationaler Galerien in dem neuen Kunstzentrum der Gillman Barracks beheimatet. Das NTU Centre for Contemporary Art Singapore verfolgt eine ganzheitliche Herangehensweise an Kunst und Kultur, indem es drei Plattformen miteinander kombiniert: Ausstellungen, Aufenthaltsstipendien und Forschung.

Koh Nguang How, The exhibition *Errata* at p-10 curatorial space (Die Ausstellung *Errata* im Kuratorenraum p-10), 2005

Koh Nguang How, Visitors to Koh's CCA residency (Besucher in Kohs CCA-Residenz), 2014

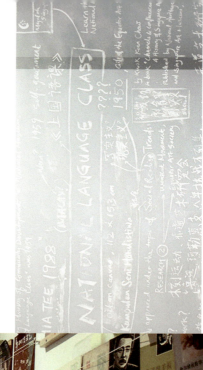

Koh Nguang How, Koh's archive at the Singapore Biennale 2013 (Kohs Archiv auf der Singapur Biennale 2013)

THE SINGAPORE ART ARCHIVE PROJECT: FROM YISHUN TO GILLMAN BARRACKS
Koh Nguang How

Beginning

The *Singapore Art Archive Project* (*SAAP*)[1] is a work-in-progress (site-specific installation work) I first initiated in 1999, when I was able to get a 3-room HDB flat[2] in Yishun New Town, after living with my parents in a 4-room flat in the same block since 1983. It was to be a private space for housing my growing collection of materials related to art and culture in Singapore and other countries that I visited since 1980. With the gathering of the materials in my own flat, I could allow overseas artists and researchers to stay. Increasingly, I started to provide materials to assist in research and projects by people in Singapore and abroad. However, the task of making these materials comprehensive and accessible for use in my tiny flat become more difficult as the flat is primarily meant for residential use.

In 1999, there was only the National Archives in Singapore, established in 1968, whose role was the keeper of records of national and historical significance, hardly focusing on artists and arts events. Incidentally in 2000, the establishment of the *Asia Art Archive*[3] in Hong Kong gave me the inspiration to work on better solutions for my archive project, with which my tiny flat was no longer able to cope.

Collection and Photography

My collection for the *Singapore Art Archive Project* began when I was a student in junior college in 1980 with newspaper clippings (English & Chinese) that were required for study purposes. I was also doing art as a subject, so naturally my focus was more on art related articles. I continue to collect the newspaper clippings till this day.

My first occupation was as Museum Assistant at the National Museum Art Gallery (NMAG)[4], Singapore, from October 1985 to January 1992. My duties were accessioning, storing and retrieving of artifacts, assisting the Assistant Curator of Art and Curator of Art in their work. The environment allowed me to meet and work with artists, curators and other people in the art world. The NMAG was a common and central place for local artists and art societies to have their shows, offering a range of events such as exhibitions, lectures, workshops and competitions. As such, my experience of art and related issues grew progressively along with my collection of related materials.

Photography was not a designated duty for me at the NMAG but an essential step in the process of artifact registration and exhibition preparation; I developed my basic knowledge of photography and started to record events such as exhibitions, opening ceremonies, press conferences, lectures, workshops and studio visits. In June 1987, I was given my first official assignment as official photographer by my curator for the

---

1. The name *Singapore Art Archive Project* was not used until 2005.
2. The Housing and Development Board (HDB) established in 1960, is the government agency responsible for Singapore's public housing programme. Today, more than 80% of Singaporeans live in HDB flats compared with only nine percent in 1960 when HDB was first established.
3. *Asia Art Archive* was initiated in Hong Kong in 2000 inresponse to the urgent need to document and secure the multiple recent histories of contemporary art in the region. Their collection now holds over 50,000 records, comprised of hundreds of thousands of physical and digital items, and it continues to grow.
4. The National Museum Art Gallery (NMAG) was established in 1976 as part of the National Museum (established in 1887), to provide modern exhibition rooms for local art and a small multi-purpose theatre, through the donations from the government and the public. It ceased to exist after the establishment of Singapore Art Museum in 1993.

Fifth *ASEAN* Youth Painting Workshop[5], which was jointly organized by The Ministry of Community Development (MCD) and The National Museum. I could observe the working methods by different Master Painters and young student artists from the six Southeast Asian countries. In August, I started my first significant photographic documentation on Performance Art; a four-day performance event by Tang Da Wu[6], entitled *Four Days at National Museum Art Gallery*. While working in a museum, the new materials in my collection expanded to include exhibition invitation cards, catalogues, posters, flyers, photographs, videos and sound recordings. I also photographed the physical changes in the rural and urban landscapes in Singapore when not at art events. I was interested in the disappearing landscapes around my new home (a HDB flat); having moved out of a village environment where I lived throughout my childhood, I tried to recover the memories through photography. Later when the villages were gone, I continued photographing the urban scenes near the *National Museum* where I worked.

Coordination and Research Jobs

I left the National Museum Art Gallery in early 1992 to become a full-time artist and I was associated with the newly registered art group The Artists Village.[7] I travelled occasionally as an artist and collected materials for the *SAAP*, from the places I visited.

In 1996, I had the opportunity to act as a coordinator for Fukuoka Art Museum in Japan, for its exhibition project *The Birth of Modern Art in South East Asia: Artists and Movements*. My involvement in the project allowed me to learn more about some older and forgotten artists, their works and the early history of Singapore art. After that Fukuoka project, I decided that my documentation priority should be the fast-disappearing old artists' works and their experiences. Older materials were collected through the old artists themselves, and sources like flea markets, second-hand bookstores, books sale, vacating buildings and garbage sites.

From Sep 1999 – Feb 2000, I was selected as a researcher in the pilot Researcher/Curator in Residence Program, at the newly established Fukuoka Asian Art Museum, Japan. The residency led to more serious collection and research into the earlier generations of artists and art activities in Singapore, including the obscure ones. So, the amount of materials on the older art history of Singapore grew; the task of digitizing and preserving the materials became a serious concern for me. By then, I realized that it was impossible for me to document and research two different courses of art history - the contemporary and the past. So, I decided to spend less of my time and resources on younger artists and future events, especially with the arrival of the internet and digital recording devices in Singapore. It resulted in a collection of close to 300 rolls of photographic films unprocessed to this day, after exposing them to arts and life events from 2002 to 2003. It started as an accumulation of films due to a lack of financial ability to process and print out the images, and then it became a work that dealt with lost memories, lost archives and the giving up of documenting future events.

5. The Association of Southeast Asian Nations (ASEAN) was established on 8 August 1967 in Bangkok, by Indonesia, Malaysia, The Philippines, Singapore, and Thailand. ASEAN was formed to promote peace and stability in the region, and to contain the spread of communism to Southeast Asian countries. Brunei Darussalam joined on 8 January 1984, Vietnam on 28 July 1995, Laos and Myanmar on 23 July 1997, and Cambodia on 30 April 1999. The Fifth ASEAN Youth Painting Workshop (and exhibition) was held in Singapore, in 1987; jointly organized by the Ministry of Community Development and the Singapore National Museum. The First ASEAN Youth Painting Workshop started in Bangkok, in 1983. The last & sixth host of the workshop series was Brunei, in 1988.
6. Tang Da Wu is a prominent contemporary artist from Singapore; he graduated with M.A. Fine Art, from *Goldsmiths College, University of London*, in 1985. He actively did performance art since his return to Singapore in 1988.
7. *The Artists Village* was founded in 1988 at some rural farm space in the northern part of Singapore as the first artists' colony for young contemporary artists. The space was acquired by the government for military use in 1990. The continuing artists officially registered the group as *The Artists Village (TAV)* in 1992. It currently continues activities without a permanent space and hosts a residency programme on an island called *Pulau Ubin* near the *Changi* International Airport.

Archives as Content and Medium of Art

In 2004, I was invited to have a solo show by a new curatorial initiative p-10, situated near Little India in Singapore, where some young artists created their studios from apartment spaces. I decided to present some of my archival materials for the new artist's community, which resulted in the *p-10* curated show *ERRATA: Page 71, Plate 47. Image caption. Change Year: 1950 to Year: 1959; Reported September 2004 by Koh Nguang How*. In short, the *ERRATA* show was based on the wrong dating of a 1959 painting by artist Chua Mia Tee of Malay language as the new National Language of the new self-governed State of Singapore, in the book *Channels & Confluences: A History of Singapore Art* written by the Director of the Singapore Art Museum Kwok Kian Chow in 1996. I presented different groups of old publications from my collection to provide clues and answers for the audiences to find the correct answer to the date of the painting. The audiences got to see and handle some rare publications in the process. The *ERRATA* show went on at two other venues in 2005: at NUS Central Library co-organised by *p-10 & University Scholars Programme*, and the Singapore History Museum. The *ERRATA* show became the start of a series of works in which I would present archival materials to the audience so that they could view them as archival resources as well as installation artwork.

After the rather well received *ERRATA* show, *p-10* invited me for a residency in 2005. From the residency room at *p-10*, I started the name *Singapore Art Archive Project (SAAP)*; and the SAAP@p-10 was then to establish a resource of archival materials on contemporary art in Singapore, using existing materials in my collection. It was for the research in the field of contemporary art in Asia and its networks. The residency project also dealt with issues concerning storage, data-entry and basic archiving practices, and lasted from January to July 2005. The networking of Singapore artists was featured in June-Aug 2005 in the exhibition *Situation: Collaborations, Collectives and Artist Networks from Sydney, Singapore and Berlin* by the Museum of Contemporary Art, Sydney, after my residency with *p-10*. I presented a timeline and archival materials of *The Artists Village*. In 2008, I also contributed my archives to the exhibition *The Artists Village: 20 Years On* at the Singapore Art Museum.

In 2011, I was invited to make a work for *Open House"*—The 3rd Singapore Biennale at 8Q at Singapore Art Museum (8Q-SAM). I took the opportunity to show my 30 years of newspaper clippings including many uncut issues. I named the installation work *Artists in the News* (also known as *SAAP@8Q-SAM*) featuring the English and Chinese morning papers mainly from 1980 to 2011. The newspapers were presented in various themes on the walls like large pin-boards and in smaller installation pieces. I highlighted a news article of the "groundbreaking" installation work by Tang Da Wu from April 1980 called *Earthworks* as a reference to the developments of the arts in Singapore and the world 30 years later. This *Earthworks*, however, was prematurely terminated by the Director of the National Museum in 1980. Ironically, a mixed media installation work *Welcome to the Hotel Munber* by Japanese-British artist Simon Fujiwara in the same biennale was censored by the Singapore Art Museum.

In 2013, the opening of the NTU Centre for Contemporary Art, Singapore (CCA)[8] in the new art enclave Gillman Barracks was officially announced. It was followed by an invitation to me, to do a residency at Gillman Barracks from July 2014 to Jan 2015. I presented the *Singapore Art Archive Project @CCA" (SAAP@CCA)* which coincided

---

8. The NTU Centre for Contemporary Art Singapore is a research centre of Nanyang Technological University, developed with support from the Economic Development Board, Singapore. It is located in the new art enclave Gillman Barracks alongside a cluster of international galleries. The NTU Centre for Contemporary Art Singapore takes a holistic approach towards art and culture, intertwining its three platforms: Exhibitions, Residencies and Research.

with the exhibition *No Country: Contemporary Art for South and Southeast Asia* at CCA, which also featured Singapore artist Tang Da Wu, whose performance art activities formed a key component of my contemporary art archives. The collection for *SAAP@CCA* is the most extensive to date, including: newspapers, invitation cards, flyers, catalogues, periodicals, posters, slide and negative films, photographs, audio recordings and original artworks. The *SAAP@CCA* would also facilitate research and collaboration between the different artists-in-residence, CCA curators, visiting curators and research fellows.

Future of Singapore Art Archive Project

The *SAAP@CCA* will eventually end when the residency was completed on 31st January 2015. These archives, dated as early as the 1920s, moved back to my residential flat and that of my parents' in Yishun. The *SAAP@CCA* awaits its next fateful host or destiny.

SINGAPUR ALS GARTENSTADT: DIE TECHNO-ORGANISCHE HEIMAT
MayEe Wong

Am 17. Juni 1963 druckte die Singapurer Zeitung The Straits Times ein Foto ab, das den Premierminister von Singapur, Lee Kuan Yew, zeigt, wie er sich am Holland Circus mit einer Gartenhacke über einen Schössling des Mempat-Baums beugt und dabei von zahlreichen Offiziellen beobachtet wird. In der begleitenden Meldung wird der Akt des Baumpflanzens durch den Staatsmann im Rahmen seiner Rundreise durch die verschiedenen ‚kampongs' (Dörfer) im Verwaltungsbezirk Ulu Pandan als Beginn einer Baumpflanz-Kampagne in ganz Singapur beschrieben, um „dazu beizutragen, Regen zu bringen".[1] Wie Lee den bescheidenen Baumtrieb einpflanzt, sollte zum ikonischen Bild für einen umfassenderen und ehrgeizigeren Plan werden, das unabhängig gewordene Land zu ästhetisieren – ein Plan, der auch die Auflösung der einst von Lee besuchten ‚kampongs' umfasste, um ein hyperurbanisiertes und ‚sauberes und grünes' Singapur aufzubauen.

Als sie 1967 die *Gartenstadt*-Kampagne ins Leben riefen, verfolgten die Führer Singapurs damit die Vision einer „schönen Gartenstadt mit Blumen und Bäumen, so sauber und abfallfrei wie nur möglich".[2] Das Gartenstadt-Konzept hat seit den 1960er Jahren Bestand. Ihm wurde eine Schlüsselrolle bei dem Schritt der Nation Singapur „von der Dritten Welt in die Erste"[3] sowie bei der Begründung ihrer Position als bedeutende globale Stadt in Südostasien zugeschrieben. Im Jahr 2013 aktualisierte die Singapurer Regierung das *Gartenstadt*-Konzept in Form der Kampagne ‚Stadt in einem Garten', das mit der Eröffnung eines riesigen Parkgeländes namens *Gardens by the Bay* inauguriert wurde. Dieser Park, der aus Freiluftgärten, zwei Gewächshäusern mit Gitternetzkuppeln und achtzehn *Supertree*-Konstruktionen besteht, wurde als „futuristische Interpretation der Natur und beeindruckende Vision der Stadt der Zukunft"[4] beschrieben. Als neuer öffentlicher Raum gestaltet, ist *Gardens by the Bay* ein Symbol, das das Engagement des Staates für die vor beinahe fünfzig Jahren aufgestellten Ideale der Gartenstadt bekräftigt.

Besucht man die Freiluftgärten von *Gardens by the Bay*, dann begegnet man der dichten Üppigkeit tropischen Grüns, das in seiner manikürten Form den Besucher niemals überfordert. Wahrscheinlich wird man eine Form des technischen Erhabenen erfahren, wenn man die *Supertrees* hinauffährt, sei es, dass man diese Konstruktionen mit ihren technischen Anlagen zur Erzeugung erneuerbarer Energie bewundert, sei es, dass man aus fünfundzwanzig Metern Höhe die perfekte Landschaftsgestaltung der Gärten erfasst. *Gardens by the Bay* repräsentiert den Höhepunkt oder gar das Überbieten der Bestrebungen der Regierung Singapurs, den Stadtstaat in eine Utopie des modernen urbanen Lebens umzuformen. Doch während wir die rasante Umwandlung Singapurs von einer *Gartenstadt* in eine *Stadt im Garten* begreifen, wollen wir das im Schnelldurchlauf erzählte Narrativ der singapurischen Erfolgsgeschichte der Stadterneuerung für einen Moment verlangsamen. Wie hat das Konzept des ‚Gartens' die Stadt Singapur geformt und wie hat es zum Wachstum Singapurs als Nation beigetragen? Schon oft wurde über die Vegetation Singapurs und seine hochmoderne Infrastruktur gesprochen, doch wie ist die Gartenstadt als Heimat für seine Bewohner eingerichtet?

---

1. The Straits Times, *Lee Begins the Tree Campaign*, 17. Juni 1963.
2. The Straits Times, *S'pore to become beautiful and clean city in three years*, 12. Mai 1967.
3. Dieser Ausdruck entstammt dem Titel von Lee Kuan Yews Buch *From Third World to First. The Singapore Story. 1965–2000, Singapore and the Asian Economic Boom*.
4. Carrie Halperin, *Changing Cities. Singapore, the Garden City*, ABC News, 22. Juli 2012,
http://abcnews.go.com/blogs/technology/2012/07/changing-cities-singapore-the-garden-city/
http://de.wikipedia.org/wiki/Gardens_by_the_Bay

Während der Ausdruck *Gartenstadt* andeutungsweise auf das Konzept der von einem Grüngürtel gesäumten, autarken Gartenstadt des Stadtvisionärs Ebenezer Howard aus dem 19. Jahrhundert verweisen mag, unterscheidet sich das Konzept der Singapurer Regierung durch das Technokratische des Ansatzes und der Durchführung von Stadtplanung und gesellschaftlicher Entwicklung. Während das Singapurer Konzept der Gartenstadt, wie bei Howard, die bewusste Einbeziehung der Vegetation in den Lebensraum umfasst, macht es Singapur als Nation nicht nur in Bezug auf den physischen Raum, sondern auch als wirksame Metapher bei der Regulierung der öffentlichen Kultur nutzbar. Die führenden Kräfte Singapurs sind „Gärtner",[5] die die Bevölkerung der Stadt im Sinne des wirtschaftlichen und nationalen Wachstums kultivieren. Der Stadtstaat wird von der Singapurer Regierung als lebendiger Organismus betrachtet; als ‚Gärtner' der Nation steckt die Regierung die Grenzen des akzeptablen sozialen Verhaltens ab, während sie maßgebliche Veränderungen der Landschaft als manipulierbare lebendige Ökologie von Organismen anordnet. Das nationale Wachstum wird von oben festgelegt, statt natürlich aus sich selbst heraus zu entstehen, indem die Regierung sowohl das soziale Leben wie die physische Umwelt, die als spiegelbildlich verstanden werden, diszipliniert, damit sie kollektiv Ordnung und Effizienz reflektieren.

Ein kleiner Hafen an der südlichsten Spitze der malaysischen Halbinsel, erlangte der Stadtstaat Singapur, der zuvor unter britischer Herrschaft gestanden hatte, 1965 die Unabhängigkeit, als er sich aus der Föderation mit Malaysia löste. Mit der schwierigen Lage der Insel konfrontiert, deren marode Wirtschaft über keinerlei nationale Ressourcen verfügte, realisierten der damalige Premierminister Lee Kuan Yew und sein Kabinett eine Politik der Industrialisierung, die darauf ausgerichtet war, ausländisches Kapital anzuziehen. Gleichzeitig setzte die Regierung Singapurs ein nationales Programm der modernisierenden Urbanisierung in Gang, das im großen Maßstab die Umsiedlung der Bevölkerung in öffentlichen Wohnungsbau in Form von Wohntürmen sowie die Säuberung der Landschaft von Slums und Dörfern umfasste. Bäume, Flora und Fauna dienten dekorativen Zwecken bei der Einrichtung einer urbanen funktionalen und effizienten Corbusier'schen Wohnmaschine. Lee und seine Minister verfolgten zwei miteinander verbundene Ziele: Zum einen sollte Singapur als attraktiver Standort für ausländische Investitionen gefördert werden; zum anderen sollte die Stadt für seine Bewohner als angenehmes Wohnumfeld eingerichtet werden, in dem sie von den Schwierigkeiten des konkreten urbanen Lebens befreit wären. Die 1967 initiierte *Gartenstadt*-Kampagne war ein zweistufiger Plan, der in den folgenden drei Jahren umgesetzt werden sollte: zunächst die Beseitigung des Mülls von den städtischen Flächen in Singapur, sodann die Erziehung der Bevölkerung bezüglich ihres Beitrags zu bürgerschaftlicher Verantwortung durch öffentliche Kampagnen und die Einführung hoher Bußgelder. Wie die Straits Times damals berichtete: „Der Premierminister betonte, dass der Standard der öffentlichen Gesundheit in Singapur als erster Indikator für die Moral und die Gesundheit des Volkes diene."[6]

Die *Gartenstadt*-Kampagne zielte darauf ab, die Singapurer dazu zu animieren, Stolz auf Singapur als ihre Heimat zu empfinden, und den Stadtstaat von seinen südostasiatischen Nachbarn als eine „Oase der Ersten Welt"[7] abzugrenzen. Die disziplinierte Bevölkerung und die saubere Umwelt in Singapur dienten als Kontrast zu der ‚Verwilderung' der benachbarten Entwicklungsländer, eine Verwilderung, die oftmals im Zusammenhang mit Problemen wie etwa dem ungleichmäßigen städtischen Wachstum

---

5. Der Direktor des Institute of Policy Studies, Janadas Devan, hielt eine in der Straits Times (21. September 2013) veröffentlichte Rede mit dem Titel „Gardeners with Guts" über Lee Kuan Yew und die Rolle der Regierung beim Aufbau von Singapur als Nation.
6. The Straits Times, *S'pore to become beautiful and clean city in three years*, 12. Mai 1967.
7. The New York Times, *Excerpts from an interview with Lee Kuan Yew*, 29. August 2007,
http://www.nytimes.com/2007/08/29/world/asia/29iht-lee-excerpts.html

und der Korruption der Bürokratie wahrgenommen wurde. Die *Gartenstadt*-Kampagne und die Nachfolgekampagne der *Stadt im Garten* haben sich für den Stadtstaat als offenbar erfolgreiche Strategie erwiesen, der heute im Index der globalen Finanzzentren von 2014 den vierten Platz hinter New York, London und Hongkong einnimmt. Im Jahr 2015 entspricht Singapur der Beschreibung als „betriebsame Metropole, die in eine üppige Hülle aus tropischer Vegetation eingebettet ist",[8] und zieht noch immer ausländische Fachleute und Superreiche an, die in Singapur leben und zu den verschiedenen wissensbasierten Ökonomien beitragen. Singapur ist nicht nur eine *Gartenstadt*, sondern eine *Stadt in einem Garten* – wobei die Stadt heute ein Knotenpunkt in dem Garten ist, der sich zu einem größeren Ökosystem ausgeweitet hat. Wie durch den Namenswechsel der Kampagnen angedeutet, weicht das energische bewusste Stutzen der Körperpolitik des Stadtstaates durch die ‚Gärtner' der Gartenstadt einer scheinbar freieren Konzeption sozioökonomischen Wachstums, bei dem die Stadt als ein Knotenpunkt innerhalb eines umfassenderen, komplexeren Überbaus der Steuerung verstanden wird, der mit dem Rest der Welt verbunden ist.

Ebenso wie die Gartenmetapher bezieht sich auch der Verweis auf die Ökologie sowohl auf die physische wie auf die soziale Umgebung. Im Aufgreifen von Figuren der Ökologie und des Organischen in den Diskursen des Unternehmertums und der Wissensindustrie hat die Singapurer Regierung den Stadtstaat als Drehkreuz für das globale „Ökosystem der Unternehmen" oder die „Ökologie der Kompetenz"[9] angepriesen. Mit dieser ökologischen Rhetorik wird die Entwicklung verschiedener technowissenschaftlicher Wissensindustrien wie etwa der Biotechnologie beschrieben, die die Anwerbung ausländischer Wissenschaftler, Unternehmer und Administratoren umfasst, die in durch singapurisches Startkapital finanzierten ‚Start-up-Unternehmen' arbeiten, sowie die Vermittlung von Singapurern in ausländische Bildungseinrichtungen zur wissenschaftlichen, technischen und wirtschaftlichen Ausbildung. Aihwa Ong weist auf die spezifische Verwendung der Gartenmetaphorik durch einen Funktionär des ECONOMIC DEVELOPMENT BOARD (EDB) hin, wenn sie ihn mit seiner Aussage zitiert, dass das EDB „Programme sät und den Dünger bereitstellt und somit als Katalysator für verschiedene Organismen dient, damit diese in dem Ökosystem" von Wagniskapital, Forschungseinrichtungen und ausländischen Experten „gedeihen."[10]

Wenn die Singapurer Regierung Singapur gleichzeitig als ‚intelligente Stadt' bewirbt, gestaltet sie damit den Stadtstaat zu einer techno-organischen Gartenstadt um. Ong stellt fest, dass die Regierung heute die Förderung von Kreativität, Innovation und Risikobereitschaft bei der ansässigen Bevölkerung anregt, und meint, dass die Gärtner damit ihren unbeholfenen Ansatz des Regierens abzuschütteln scheinen. Doch während Singapur ein beträchtliches Wirtschaftswachstum erreicht hat, lässt sich vom Wachstum des Staatsvolks kaum dasselbe behaupten. Singapur ist für seine niedrige nationale Geburtenrate[11] ebenso berüchtigt wie für die staatlichen Versuche, die Singapurer davon zu überzeugen versuchen, sich fortzupflanzen.[12] Die Regierung hat sich der Immigration zugewendet, um den Effekten der niedrigen Geburtenrate entgegenzuwirken. Singapurische Staatsbürger machen heute etwa 61% der Gesamtbevölkerung Singapurs aus.[13] Dieses Szenario hat die Bewohner Singapurs

---

8. Yong Soon Tan, Tung Jean Lee, Karen Tan, *Clean, Green and Blue. Singapore's Journey Towards Environmental and Water Sustainability*, Singapore: ISEAS Publishing, 2009, S. 221.
9. Aihwa Ong, „*Intelligent Island, Baroque Ecology, in Beyond Description. Singapore Space Historicity*", hg. von Ryan Bishop, John Phillips und Wei-wei Yeo, London: Routledge, 2004, S. 178.
10. Ebd.
11. Die zusammengefasste Geburtenziffer der Einwohner beträgt im Jahr 2013 1,19, gemäß der Veröffentlichung *2014 Population in Brief*, herausgegeben von der *National Population and Talent Division (NPTD)* der Singapurer Regierung. Letzter Zugriff am 21. Januar 2015, http://www.nptd.gov.sg/portals/0/homepage/highlights/population-in-brief-2014.pdf
12. Kate Hodal, *Singapore uses ‚modern fairytales' to warn women of declining fertility*, The Guardian, 22. März 2013, http://www.theguardian.com/world/2013/mar/22/singapore-fairytales-warn-declining-fertility
13. Diese Zahl basiert auf folgenden Angaben: Staatsbürger (3,34 Mio.), unbefristet Aufenthaltsberechtigte (0,53 Mio.), Ausländer (1,6 Mio.), Gesamtbevölkerung Stand Juni 2014 (5,47 Mio.). *2014 Population in Brief*, a.a.O., S. 5.

zu der Frage geführt: Für wen stellt Singapur tatsächlich eine Heimat dar? Singapurer haben ihre Unzufriedenheit mit Ausländern und Immigranten zum Ausdruck gebracht, was in einigen Fällen fremdenfeindliche Ausmaße erreicht hat.[14] Diese Stimmungen verraten soziale Spannungen, die die Ideologie des singapurischen Techno-Organischen unterminieren: dass alles, was in Singapur gepflanzt oder dorthin verpflanzt wird, durch bloßen Willen und Ingenieurskunst wachsen wird.

Gardens by the Bay, die jüngste architektonische Ikone Singapurs, ist emblematisch für diese techno-organische Ideologie. Die Gewächshäuser mit den Gitternetzkuppeln sollen Pflanzengattungen aus „Habitats auf der ganzen Welt, die durch den Klimawandel am meisten gefährdet sind",[15] unter klimatisierten Bedingungen beherbergen. Die Gärten beeindrucken uns hier dadurch, dass sie die Künstlichkeit des Klimas hervorheben und die Fähigkeit von Design und Ingenieurswesen betonen, durch die diese fremden Pflanzen so weit entfernt von ihrem einheimischen Umfeld gedeihen können. Auch die *Supertree*-Konstruktionen – acht Meter hohe vertikale Gärten – erfüllen uns mit Ehrfurcht als Meisterleistungen des Ingenieurswesen. Wie der Architekt Paul Baker bei einer Diskussion über die Gestaltung der Gärten kommentierte, ist „an Singapur ziemlich erstaunlich, dass die Dinge wirklich wachsen."[16] Während vertikale Anpflanzungen anderswo „viel Bewässerung und viel Arbeit" erfordern, konnten die Architekten im Fall der *Supertrees* „Dinge in die Luft hängen, und sie überlebten."[17] Doch während Pflanzen in kontrollierten Umgebungen gedeihen mögen, ist weniger gewiss, ob auch Menschen sich auf ähnliche Weise verhalten. Eine Frage bleibt: Kann ein Ökosystem zur Heimat werden?

---

14. Mark Fenn, *Singapore's Foreigner Problem*, The Diplomat, 21. Februar 2014, http://thediplomat.com/2014/02/singapores-foreigner-problem/
15. WilkinsonEyre Architects, *Gardens By the Bay, Singapore*,
http://www.wilkinsoneyre.com/projects/singapore-gardens-by-the-bay.aspx?category=sport-and-leisure
16. „We wanted real drama in a flat landscape' – Paul Baker on Gardens by the Bay", *Dezeen magazine*, 4. November 2012,
http://www.dezeen.com/2012/11/04/we-wanted-to-create-real-drama-in-a-very-flat-landscape-paul-baker-on-gardens-by-the-bay/
17. Ebd.

SINGAPORE AS GARDEN CITY: THE TECHNO-ORGANIC HOME
MayEe Wong

On 17th of June, 1963, the Singaporean newspaper The Straits Times featured a photograph of the Prime Minister of Singapore, Lee Kuan Yew, bent over a sampling of the Mempat tree with a hoe at Holland Circus, as he is watched by numerous officials. The accompanying report describes the statesman's tree-planting act as inaugurating a tree-planting campaign across Singapore "to help bring rain",[1] as part of his tour of the various 'kampongs' (i.e. rural villages) in the Ulu Pandan political constituency. Lee's planting of the modest tree sapling would become the iconic image for a larger, more ambitious plan to aestheticise the newly independent country—a plan that would involve clearing away the *kampongs* Lee had once visited to build up a hyper-urbanised and 'clean and green' Singapore.

Launching the *Garden City* campaign in 1967, Singapore's leaders envisioned Singapore as "a garden city beautiful with flowers and trees, and as tidy and litterless as it can be."[2] Since the 1960s, the *Garden City* concept has endured. It has been credited as a key factor in Singapore's leap from its "Third World to First"[3] nation status, and in establishing its position as a prominent global city in Southeast Asia. In 2013, the Singaporean government updated the *Garden City* concept in the form of the *City in a Garden* campaign, headlined by the unveiling of a superpark, *Gardens by the Bay*. Consisting of outdoor gardens, two gridshell domed conservatories and eighteen Supertree structures, *Gardens by the Bay* has been described as a "futuristic take on nature and as well as an awe-inspiring vision for the future of a city."[4] Designed as a new civic space, *Gardens by the Bay* is a symbol affirming the government's commitment to the ideals of the *Garden City* laid out nearly fifty years before.

If you visit the outdoor gardens of the *Gardens by the Bay*, you will encounter the dense lushness of tropical greenery, which is never too overwhelming for the visitor in its manicured form. You will probably experience a form of technological sublime if you take a ride up the Supertrees, whether marveling at these structures which hold engineering mechanisms that generate renewable energy, or taking in the immaculate landscaping of the gardens from twenty-five feet above. The *Gardens by the Bay* represents the culmination or even the surpassing of the Singaporean government's desires to mould the city-state into a utopia for modern urban living. But as we apprehend Singapore's rapid transformation from a *Garden City* to a *City in a Garden*, let us slow down the fast-forwarded narrative of the Singapore urban development success story. How has the concept of the Garden shaped the city of Singapore, and how has the concept contributed to Singapore's growth as a nation? Much has been said about Singapore's greenery and its state of the art infrastructure, but how is the garden city configured as a home for its people?

While the term *Garden City* might be suggestively allusive of urban visionary Ebenezer Howard's 19th century notion of the green-belted self-sufficient *Garden City*, the Singaporean government's notion of the *Garden City* is a different concept in the government's technocratic approach and execution to urban planning and civic development. While the Singaporean *Garden City* concept involves the deliberate incorporation of greenery into living space like Howard's, it harnesses Singapore as

---

1. The Straits Times, *Lee Begins the Tree Campaign*, June 17, 1963.
2. The Straits Times, *S'pore to become beautiful and clean city in three years*, May 12, 1967.
3. This is a phrase taken from the title of Lee Kuan Yew's book *From Third World to First: The Singapore Story: 1965 – 2000, Singapore and the Asian Economic Boom*.
4. Carrie Halperin, *Changing Cities: Singapore, the Garden City*, ABC News, July 22, 2012, http://abcnews.go.com/blogs/technology/2012/07/changing-cities-singapore-the-garden-city/.

a nation not only in terms of physical space, but also as an operative metaphor in regulating its public culture. Singapore's leaders are 'gardeners'[5] cultivating the city's population towards the outcomes of economic and national growth. The city-state is regarded as a living organism by the Singaporean government; as 'gardeners' of the nation, the government demarcates the boundaries of acceptable social behaviour, while it enacts decisive changes to the landscape as a manipulable living ecology of organisms. National growth is defined from above and not naturally on its own, with the government disciplining both social life and physical environment to mirror each other, collectively reflecting order and efficiency.

A small port city-state at the southern-most tip of the Malay Peninsula previously under British colonial rule, Singapore gained political sovereignty in 1965 when it broke away from a merger with Malaysia. Faced with the island state's vulnerable predicament of having no natural resources and an ailing economy, then-Prime Minister Lee Kuan Yew and his Cabinet implemented policies of industrialisation geared towards attracting foreign investment. At the same time, the Singaporean government instituted a national programme of modernising urbanisation that involved relocating its population into mass public housing in the form of high-rise flats, and clearing the landscape of slums and rural villages. Trees, flora and fauna served a decorative purpose in framing an urban functional and efficient Corbusian 'Machine for Living'. Lee and his ministers had two connected goals: one was to promote Singapore as an attractive place for foreign investment; the other was to establish Singapore as a pleasant city for Singaporeans to live in, relieving Singaporeans from the challenges of concrete urban life. The *Garden City* campaign, launched in 1967, was a two-staged plan for the following three years: beginning with the cleaning of rubbish from Singapore's spaces, then the education of the public on their contributions towards civic responsibility through public campaigns and the institution of heavy fines. As The Straits Times reported at the time: "[t]he Prime Minister stressed that Singapore's standard of public health served as a first indicator of the morale and health of the population."[6]

The *Garden City* campaign aimed to encourage Singaporeans to take pride in Singapore as their home, and to distinguish the city-state from the rest of its Southeast Asian neighbours as a "first-world oasis."[7] Singapore's disciplined population and clean environment served as a contrast to the 'wildness' of its developing neighbours, a wildness often perceived in problems such as uneven urban growth and bureaucratic corruption. The *Garden City* campaign and its successor, the *City in a Garden* campaign, have arguably been a successful strategy for the city-state, which now occupies fourth place in the 2014 Global Financial Centres Index behind New York, London and Hong Kong. In 2015, Singapore fits the description of "a bustling metropolis nestled in a lush mantle of tropical greenery",[8] and it continues to attract foreign professionals and high net-worth individuals to live in Singapore as contributors to its various knowledge-based economies. Singapore is not just a *garden city*, but a *city in a garden*—with the city now a node in the garden, which has expanded into a larger ecological system. As suggested in the shift of campaign names, the forceful deliberate pruning of the city-state body politic by the 'gardeners' of the garden city gives way to a seemingly freer conception of socio-economic growth, with the

---

5. Institute of Policy Studies director Janadas Devan gave a speech published in The Straits Times (September 21, 2013), titled *Lee Kuan Yew and the Singaporean government's role's in building Singapore as a nation*.
6. The Straits Times, *S'pore to become beautiful and clean city in three years*, May 12, 1967.
7. The New York Times, *Excerpts from an interview with Lee Kuan Yew*, August 29, 2007, http://www.nytimes.com/2007/08/29/world/asia/29iht-lee-excerpts.html.
8. Yong Soon Tan, Tung Jean Lee, Karen Tan, *Clean, Green and Blue: Singapore's Journey Towards Environmental and Water Sustainability*, Singapore: ISEAS Publishing, 2009, p. 221.

city conceived as a node within a larger, more sophisticated superstructure of governance that is connected to the rest of the world.

Like the garden metaphor, the ecology reference applies to both the physical environment, and the social environment. Adopting tropes of ecology and organicity in entrepreneurial and knowledge industry discourses, the Singaporean government has been promoting the city-state as a hub of the global 'enterprise eco-system', or the 'ecology of expertise.'[9] This ecological rhetoric is used to describe the development of various technoscientific knowledge industries, such as those of biotechnology, which involves attracting foreign scientists, entrepreneurs and administrators to work in start-up companies funded by Singaporean seed money, and the placement of Singaporeans in foreign educational institutions for training in science, engineering and business. Aihwa Ong notes the specific use of the gardening metaphor by an official at the Economic Development Board (EDB) in citing how the EDB "seeds schemes and provides the fertilizers, acting as a catalyst for different organisms to thrive in the ecosystem"[10] of venture capitalism, research institutes and foreign experts.

The Singaporean government's simultaneous promotion of Singapore as an 'intelligent city' recasts the city-state as a *Techno-Organic Garden City*. Ong notes that the Singaporean government now encourages the fostering of creativity, innovation and risk-taking in the local population, suggesting that the gardeners are now seemingly shaking off their heavy-handed approach to governance. But while Singapore has achieved considerable economic growth, less could be said for the growth of the citizen population. Singapore is notorious for its low national birthrate,[11] and for the government's attempts to persuade Singaporeans to procreate.[12] The government has turned to immigration to counter the effects of the low birthrate. To date, Singaporean citizens constitute about 61% of the total Singaporean population.[13] This scenario has led resident Singaporeans to question: for whom is Singapore really a home? Singaporeans have expressed their discontent with foreigners and immigrants, which, in some cases, have reached xenophobic extents.[14] These sentiments betray social tensions that undermine the ideology of Singaporean techno-organicity: that through sheer will and engineering, anything planted or transplanted in Singapore will grow.

Gardens by the Bay, the most recent architectural icon of Singapore, is emblematic of this techno-organic ideology. The gridshell dome conservatories of the Gardens are designed to house plant species from "world habitats most at risk from climate change"[15] in climate-controlled conditions. Here, the Gardens impress us by foregrounding the artificiality of the climate and highlighting the power of design and engineering in enabling these foreign plants to thrive so far away from their endemic environments. The Supertree structures—twenty-five feet tall vertical gardens—likewise,

---

9. Aihwa Ong, *Intelligent Island, Baroque Ecology, in Beyond Description: Singapore Space Historicity*, edited by Ryan Bishop, John Phillips and Wei-wei Yeo, London: Routledge, 2004, p. 178.
10. Ibid.
11. The Resident total fertility rate for 2013 is 1.19, according to *2014 Population in Brief*, published by the National Population and Talent Division (NPTD) of the Singapore Government. Last accessed, 21 January 2015, http://www.nptd.gov.sg/portals/0/homepage/highlights/population-in-brief-2014.pdf.
12. Kate Hodal, *Singapore uses 'modern fairytales' to warn women of declining fertility*, The Guardian, 22 March 2013, http://www.theguardian.com/world/2013/mar/22/singapore-fairytales-warn-declining-fertility#.
13. This figure is based on these statistics: Citizens (3.34m), Permanent Residents (0.53m), Non-Residents (1.6m), total population as of June 2014 (5.47 m). 2014 *Population in Brief*, 5.
14. Mark Fenn, *Singapore's Foreiger Problem, The Diplomat*, 21 February 2014, http://thediplomat.com/2014/02/singapores-foreigner-problem/.
15. WilkinsonEyre Architects, *Gardens By the Bay, Singapore*, http://www.wilkinsoneyre.com/projects/singapore-gardens-by-the-bay.aspx?category=sport-and-leisure.

awe us as engineering feats. As architect Paul Baker has commented while discussing the design of the Gardens, "[o]ne of the rather amazing things about Singapore is that things do grow."[16] While vertical planting elsewhere involves "a lot of irrigation and a lot of work," in the case of the Supertrees, the architects could "put things in the air and get them to survive."[17] But while plants may flourish in controlled environments, one is less certain that people might act in a similar way. One question remains: can an ecosystem grow to become a home?

---

16. "We wanted real drama in a flat landscape" – *Paul Baker on Gardens by the Bay*, Dezeen magazine, 4 November 2012, http://www.dezeen.com/2012/11/04/we-wanted-to-create-real-drama-in-a-very-flat-landscape-paul-baker-on-gardens-by-the-bay/.
17. Ibid.

WIR SIND ALLE *FREMDE*
Anca Rujoiu

Wie definiert uns ein Ort, lassen wir uns von einem Ort definieren? Es gibt viele verschiedene Art und Weisen, wie unsere Identität im Verhältnis zum Ort ausgedrückt werden kann, die zwischen feststehenden und subjektiven Formen der Identifikation oszillieren. Der Geburtsort, der Wohnort, der Arbeitsort, der Ort, an dem unser Pass ausgestellt wurde, der Ort, an dem unsere Eltern geboren wurden, bis hin zu prägenden Erinnerungen, die uns weniger als Bürger denn als Individuen geformt haben – der Ort, an dem wir zur Schule gegangen sind, der Ort, an dem wir als Kinder gespielt haben, der Ort, an dem wir das erste Mal unseren Freund getroffen haben. Was die modernen Nationalstaaten mit ihren Klassifikationssystemen oftmals anzuerkennen und zu erfassen versäumen, ist, dass wir einer Vielzahl von Orten zugehören. Das Verhältnis zwischen Individuum–Ort–Nation ist vielschichtig und nicht feststehend; es ist ein Prozess des Werdens statt ein erstarrtes Bild. „Rose war ihr Name und wäre sie Rose wenn ihr Name nicht Rose gewesen wäre. Sie dachte nach und dann dachte sie wieder nach. Wäre sie Rose wenn ihr Name nicht Rose gewesen wäre?"[1]

In welcher Beziehung steht man zu einem Ort, von dem man überhaupt nichts weiß? Wie wird man an einem Ort heimisch, an dem man gerade angekommen ist, wenn das Abreisedatum noch nicht feststeht? Wie lange im Voraus sollte man über einen Ort Bescheid wissen, bevor man dort seinen Fuß auf den Boden setzt? Dieses Dilemma steht für mich, als Kuratorin, die vor kurzem an einen neuen Ort umgesiedelt ist, in einem gewissen Zusammenhang mit der Erfahrung eines Ausstellungsbesuchs. Wann ist der geeignete Augenblick, um die Presseinformation und/oder den Saaltext zu lesen? Üblicherweise heißen solche „Kollateral"-Kommunikationen die Besucher am Eingang zum Ausstellungsraum buchstäblich willkommen. Man wird von der Aufsichtsperson in der Galerie begrüßt, die einem die Presseinformationen überreicht, während die ersten Schritte einen zum Ausstellungstext führen, der das Wesentliche der Ausstellung auf wenige Zeilen komprimiert und den Besucher von der Aufgabe befreit, jene beklemmende Frage zu beantworten: „Wovon handelt die Ausstellung?" Die physische Platzierung des Ausstellungstexts – fast immer in der Nähe des Eingangs zur Ausstellung – bestimmt den Grundtenor der Ausstellungserfahrung. Der Ausstellungstext legitimiert das kuratorische Narrativ und verengt dabei das Verständnis der Ausstellung oft auf eine einzige Perspektive. Darüber hinaus vermittelt er eine Ausstellung lediglich auf textlicher Ebene, wodurch sie ihrer Wahrnehmung als räumliche Erfahrung beraubt wird, die an sich schon den Aufwand bestätigt, die Ausstellung zu besuchen. Vielleicht sollten wir uns der Ausstellung einfach überlassen.

Wenn wir uns an einem neuen Ort befinden, verwandeln wir uns in Teilzeit-Anthropologen.[2] Wir streifen durch die Straßen mit begutachtender Neugier und erkunden die Gebräuche und die sozialen Rituale um uns herum. Die Erwartung, erklären zu können, wovon eine Ausstellung handelt, korrespondiert mit derselben Erwartung, Wissen über einen Ort zu erwerben. Dadurch können wir oft zu einem singulären Narrativ geführt werden, das von der objektiven, allwissenden Stimme eines Erzählers verkündet wird. Dies ist die Stimme, die eine Filmemacherin wie Trinh T. Minh-ha in ihren Filmen ablehnt, da sie das herkömmliche positivistische Programm, den Bildern eine Bedeutung zu verleihen, ablehnt. „Wissen von etwas gibt oft die Illusion von Wissen."[3]

---

1. Gertrude Stein, *Die Welt ist rund*, Klagenfurt: Ritter, 2001.
2. Julia Kristeva, *Fremde sind wir uns selbst*, Frankfurt/M.: Suhrkamp, 1990.
3. Trinh T. Minh-ha, *When the Moon Waxes Red. Representation, Gender and Cultural Politics*, New York: Routledge, 1991, S. 65.

Über das gesamte Spektrum der Arbeitswelt verteilt, bilden ausländische Arbeitnehmer einen erheblichen und wachsenden Anteil der Bevölkerung Singapurs.[4] Der Gesamtanteil ausländischer Arbeitskräfte macht beinahe 40% von Singapurs erwerbstätiger Bevölkerung aus, und dies auf einer Insel, deren Geschichte und Verlauf des Wirtschaftswachstums durch mehrere Einwanderungswellen geprägt wurde. Die Komplexitäten der Migration widersetzen sich einem vereinheitlichenden Bild; es handelt sich um einen vielschichtigen Prozess – dazu gehören zum Beispiel Gegensätze zwischen gering qualifizierten Arbeitern und „ausländischen Talenten",[5] in letzter Zeit aber auch Bekundungen von Unzufriedenheit über die Pläne der Regierung, die Bevölkerungszahl zu vergrößern und in diesem dicht bevölkerten Stadtstaat neue Ströme von Immigranten zuzulassen.[6] Doch ungeachtet der herkömmlichen Unterscheidungen zwischen Fremden und Einheimischen gibt es oftmals Schnittstellen und Überschneidungen, insbesondere im Fall der mittleren und unteren Schichten.

Die Definition des Fremden, so schreibt Julia Kristeva, wird immer mit Bezug auf den Begriff von Macht und auf das Verhältnis dieser Individuen zu den Mächten konstruiert. In den meisten Fällen hat der Fremde keine politischen Rechte und lebt oft in politischer Isolation. In Singapur dürfen Nicht-Singapurer keine Demonstrationen abhalten oder an Veranstaltungen und Aktivitäten zu innenpolitischen Angelegenheiten teilnehmen, selbst wenn diese in Innenräumen oder an der Speaker's Corner[7] stattfinden. Selbst für die lokale Bevölkerung stellt die Organisation und Teilnahme an öffentlichen Protesten oftmals eine schwierige Angelegenheit dar, wodurch fraglich wird, in welchem Maße sich ein Staatsbürger aktiv am politischen Leben beteiligen kann.

Ein Fremder hat oftmals ein genaueres Bewusstsein als der Durchschnittsbürger. Die obsessive Überwachung, die Sorge, etwas Falsches zu sagen oder sich unangemessen zu verhalten, die Furcht, sich in eine peinliche Lage zu bringen, versetzt den Fremden in einen ständigen Prozess der Selbstkontrolle und Selbstzensur. Der oder die Fremde beobachtet sich selbst und weiß dabei ganz genau, dass er oder sie auch beobachtet wird. Lebt man als Fremde an einem Ort wie Singapur, dann stellt man fest, dass eine solche Praxis der Selbstüberwachung auch bei der lokalen Bevölkerung verbreitet ist und von ihr betrieben wird. Dies hat mit einem gewissen latenten Bewusstsein dessen zu tun, was zu sagen erlaubt ist, aber auch mit Mechanismen der Überwachung, die selbst von jenen übernommen wurden, die keine Machtposition einnehmen. Ein einschlägiges Beispiel ist STOMP, kurz für „Straits Times Online Mobile Print", eine staatlich betriebene Plattform des Bürgerjournalismus, die den Nutzern erlaubt, direkt Geschehnisse einzustellen, was oft bedeutet: von Nutzern eingefangene Momente privater und öffentlicher Aktivitäten der Bürger, die womöglich gegen soziale Normen verstoßen oder für gesellschaftlich unerwünschte Verhaltensformen „werben."

Gibt es überhaupt glückliche Fremde? Diese Frage stellt Julia Kristeva in der Einleitung zu ihrem Buch *Fremde sind wir uns selbst*. Angetrieben von der Hoffnung, ein zukünftiges gelobtes Land zu erreichen, und gefangen in der Sehnsucht nach einem verlorenen Paradies, findet die Fremde niemals physische und emotionale Ruhe. Sie füllt die Gegenwart niemals vollständig aus, wechselt beständig zwischen Vergangenheit

---

4. http://www.singstat.gov.sg/docs/default-source/default-document-library/publications/publications_and_papers/population_and_population_structure/population2014.pdf (letzter Zugriff: 26. Februar 2015).
5. http://www.migrationpolicy.org/article/rapid-growth-singapores-immigrant-population-brings-policy-challenges (letzter Zugriff: 26. Februar 2015).
6. http://www.bbc.co.uk/news/world-asia-21485729 (letzter Zugriff: 26. Februar 2015).
7. Die Speaker's Corner ist Singapurs erster und einziger Ort im Freien, an dem Bürger öffentliche Reden halten können, ohne eine Public Entertainment Licence (Vergnügungserlaubnis) erwerben zu müssen. Nur Singapurer und Aufenthaltsberechtigte dürfen an den dort stattfindenden Demonstrationen teilnehmen oder sie organisieren.

und Zukunft hin und her. Die Gegenwart wird als fragil und veränderlich begriffen, als Übergangsmoment hin zu etwas Besserem. Als junge Nation im ständigen Prozess des Aufbaus und der Aufwertung verortet Singapur sich selbst an der Schwelle zur Zukunft, wo die Hoffnungen auf ein besseres Leben die Bereitschaft, Werte, Denk- und Lebensweisen zu opfern, bestätigen. Und doch wurden diese Erwartungen politisch und kulturell konstruiert, sodass die Hoffnungen auf soziale Mobilität und finanzielle Erfolge sich mit den Plänen der Regierung verbanden. Zerrissen zwischen der Nostalgie nach einer jüngsten, verlorenen Vergangenheit und der Hoffnung auf eine bessere Zukunft, sind wir beide – die Fremde und der Einheimische – in dieselbe Falle geraten?

Singapur, das in diesem Jahr das 50. Jubiläum seiner Unabhängigkeit feiert, ist noch immer dabei, einen Sinn von nationaler Identität bei seiner Bevölkerung zu schaffen. Eine der Strategien bestand in der Entwicklung nationaler Symbole, die allen Singapurern ein gemeinsames kulturelles Erbe und ein Gefühl der Zugehörigkeit verleihen können. Erstaunlich ist hierbei, wie dieser Prozess auch wirtschaftlichen Erwägungen folgt, sowie die Überschneidung von nationalen und touristischen Symbolen. Dies gilt zum Beispiel für Merlion, der sichtbarsten Ikonografie Singapurs, „Halbbestie", „Halbfisch", die 1964 vom Singapurer Tourismusverband entwickelt wurde.[8] Merlion selbst, eine hybride Ikone, die diverse Mythen, Symbole und historische Linien integriert, entwickelte sich von einem touristischen Emblem zu einem nationalen Symbol.[9] Ein solcher Prozess macht deutlich, dass „Repräsentationen des ‚Selbst', die zur Konsumption durch signifikante ‚Andere' entworfen werden, die Möglichkeiten und Parameter von Identitäten in dem endlosen dialogischen Spiel und den gegenseitigen Durchdringungen zwischen ‚Selbst' und ‚Anderem' definieren können."[10] Angetrieben von den Kräften des Marktes, werden kulturelle Schichten beständig in einem Ausmaß neu geschrieben, dass der Einheimische und der Tourist oftmals die Position wechseln oder sich überlagern.

Singapur ist in vielerlei Hinsicht ein Labor, ein Schwellenraum, der die Erfahrung von Fremdheit verallgemeinert und ein Bewusstsein für die umfassenderen Wirklichkeiten schafft. Ein Fremder zu sein, ist eine Position, die wir – der Außenstehende und der Einheimische – immer in uns tragen, sei es zu Hause oder im Ausland; es ist ein Prozess mit unbestimmtem Ende, durch den wir die Widersprüche und Veränderungen in uns selbst anerkennen. „Auf befremdliche Weise ist der Fremde in uns selbst […]. [Der Fremde] entsteht […], wenn in mir das Bewusstsein meiner Differenz auftaucht, und er hört auf zu bestehen, wenn wir uns alle als Fremde erkennen, widerspenstig gegen Bindungen und Gemeinschaften."[11]

---

8. Brenda S. A. Yeoh, T. C. Chang, *The rise of the merlion. Monument and Myth in the Making of the Singapore Story*, in: *Theorizing the Southeast Asian City as Text. Urban Landscapes, Cultural Documents, and Interpretative Experiences*, S. 31.
9. Ebd., S. 34.
10. Ebd., S. 39.
11. Julia Kristeva, *Fremde sind wir uns selbst*, a.a.O., S. 11.

WE ARE ALL FOREIGNERS
Anca Rujoiu

In how many ways does a place define us, do we let ourselves be defined by a place? There is an array of modalities through which our identity is articulated in relation to place, oscillating between forms of identification that are fixed and those that are subjective. The place of birth, the place of residency, the place of work, the place where our passport was issued, the place where our parents were born and moving forward to formative memories that shaped us not so much as citizens, but as individuals—the place we went to school, the place where we used to play as kids, the place where we first met our lover. What the modern nation-states often fail to acknowledge and encompass in their classification systems is that we do belong to many places. The relation between individual-place-nation is contingent and multi-layered rather than fixed; it is a process of becoming rather than a frozen picture. "Rose was her name and would she have been Rose if her name had not been Rose. She used to think and then she used to think again. Would she have been Rose if her name had not been Rose?"[1]

How does one relate to a place one doesn't know anything about? How does one unpack a place where one has just landed, with the departure date yet to be settled? How much should one know in advance about a place before setting foot on its solid ground? It is a dilemma which, for a curator like myself, recently relocated in a new place, has a certain correlation with the experience of exhibition viewing. When is a good time to read the press release and/or the exhibition wall text? Conventionally such communication 'collaterals' literally welcome the visitor at the very entrance to the exhibition space. The gallery invigilator greets you, handing over the press release while your first steps lead you towards the exhibition text, which concentrates within a few line the essence of a show, liberating the visitor from the mission of having to answer the oppressive question—"What is the show about?" The physical placement of the exhibition text—most commonly in proximity to the exhibition's entrance—sets the tone of the exhibition experience. The exhibition text legitimizes the curatorial narrative while often reducing the reading of a show to one single perspective. In addition, the exhibition text communicates a show only at a textual level, depriving the exhibition of its reception as a spatial experience that inherently validates the effort of seeing the show. Perhaps we should simply immerse ourselves in the show.

When we are in a new place, we turn ourselves into part-time anthropologists.[2] We walk into the streets with an examining curiosity and explore the habits and social rituals around us. The expectation of receiving an explaination of what a show is about corresponds to the same expectation of gaining knowledge of a place. This can often lead to us to a singular narrative delivered by the objective, omniscient voice of a narrator. This is the voice that a filmmaker such as Trinh T. Minh-ha rejects in her films, eschewing the conventional positivist routine to assign meaning to images. *Knowledge about often gives the illusion of knowledge.*[3]

From high to low ends of the labour spectrum, foreign workers constitute a significant and increasing proportion of Singapore's population.[4] The total foreign work-force makes up close to 40% of Singapore's total working population, on an island whose history and path of economic growth has been shaped by several waves of migration.

---

1. Gertrude Stein, *The World is Round*, Belgium: Esperluete Editions 2011, p. 12.
2. Julia Kristeva, *Strangers to Ourselves*, New York: Columbia University Press, 1991.
3. Trinh T. Minh-ha, *When the Moon Waxes Red: Representation, Gender and Cultural Politics*, New York: Routledge, 1991, p. 65.
4. http://www.singstat.gov.sg/docs/default-source/default-document-library/publications/publications_and_papers/population_and_population_structure/population2014.pdf (last accessed on 26 February 2015)

The complexities of migration resist a totalizing picture; it is a multi-layered process—this includes, for instance, discrepancies between low skilled workers and 'foreign talents',[5] but also recent expressions of discontent towards the government plan to increase the size of the total population, allowing new flows of immigrants in this highly dense city-state.[6] However, despite the conventional distinctions between foreigners and locals, there are often points of intersection and overlap, especially when it comes to the middle and lower local classes.

The definition of the foreigner, notes Julia Kristeva, is always constructed around the notion of power and how such individuals situate themselves in relation to forces of power. In most of the cases, the foreigner does not have political rights and often lives in political isolation. In Singapore, non-Singaporeans cannot hold demonstrations or participate in events and activities related to domestic political affairs, even in indoor spaces or at Speaker's Corner.[7] Even for the local population, organizing and taking part in a public protest is often a more difficult matter, which calls into question the extent to which a local citizen can actively take part in the political life.

A foreigner is often more self-aware, than the average citizen. The obsessive vigilance, the concern with not speaking or behaving inappropriately, the fear of embarrassing oneself, puts the foreigner into a constant state of self-monitoring and self-censorship. The foreigner watches herself as much as she knows she is being watched. As a foreigner living in a place like Singapore, one notices that such a practice of self-surveillance is spread among and conducted by the wider local population itself. This has to do with a certain latent consciousness of what one is allowed to say, but also with mechanisms of surveillance that have been taken over by those who are not in a position of authority. A relevant example is STOMP, or Straits Times Online Mobile Print, a citizen-journalism platform established by the government allowing users to post stories directly, which often means user-captured moments of citizens private and public activities that arguably contravene social norms or 'promote' socially undesirable forms of behaviours.

Are there any happy foreigners? asks Julia Kristeva in the introduction to her book *Strangers to Ourselves*. Driven by the hope of reaching a future promised land and trapped in the nostalgia for a lost paradise, the foreigner never finds herself at rest physically or emotionally. She never fully inhabits the present, she is constantly shifting between past and future. The present is conceived of as fragile and fluctuating, a transitory moment towards something better. As a young nation in a constant process of building and up-grading, Singapore situates itself on the brink of the future, where the aspirations for a better life validate the willingness to sacrifice different values, ways of thinking and living. Such aspirations have nevertheless been politically and culturally constructed, so that the hopes for social mobility and financial achievement coalesce with governmental planning. Torn between the nostalgia for a recent, lost past and the aspiration towards a brighter future, are we both—the foreigner and the local—caught in the same trap?

Celebrating its 50th year of independence this year, Singapore is still in the process of building a sense of national identity amongst its population. One strategy has been the development of national symbols that can provide all Singaporeans with a shared cultural heritage and sense of belonging. What is striking is how such a

---

5. http://www.migrationpolicy.org/article/rapid-growth-singapores-immigrant-population-brings-policy-challenges (last accessed on 26 February 2015)
6. http://www.bbc.co.uk/news/world-asia-21485729 (last accessed on 26 February 2015)
7. It is Singapore's first and only designated outdoor venue where its citizens can give public speeches without having to apply for the Public Entertainment License. Only Singaporeans and permanent residents can organize and take part in demonstrations held there.

process is also economically driven and the overlap that exists between national symbols and tourism symbols. This is the case, for instance, of the Merlion, the most visible iconography of Singapore, the "half-beast", "half-fish" conceived in 1964 by the Singapore Tourism Board.[8] Merlion itself, a hybrid icon incorporating various myths, symbols and his- torical trajectories, progressed from a tourist emblem to a national symbol.[9] Such a process highlights that "representation of 'self' projected for the consumption of significant 'others' may return to define the possibilities and parameters of identities in the endless dialogic play and interpenetrations between 'self' and 'other'."[10] Cultural layers are constantly rewritten and driven by the market forces to an extent that the local and the tourist often swap positions and overlap.

Singapore is in many ways a laboratory, a liminal space that evens out the experience of foreignness and makes you aware of wider realities. Being a foreigner is a position that we—the outsider and the local—always carry within ourselves, whether at home or abroad; it is an open-ended process through which we acknowledge the contradictions and changes within ourselves. "Strangely, the foreigner lives within us. […] The foreigner comes in when the consciousness of my difference arises, and he disappears when we all acknowledge ourselves as foreigners, unamenable to bonds and communities."[11]

8. Brenda S.A. Yeoh and T.C. Chang, *The Rise of the Merlion': Monument and Myth in the Making of Singapore Story* in *Theorising the Southeast Asian City as Text*, Singapore: World Scientific Publishing, 2003, p. 31
9. Ibid, p. 34
10. Ibid, p. 39
11. Julia Kristeva, *Strangers to Ourselves,* New York: Columbia University Press, 1991, p. 1.

THE UNHOMELY IS
THE SHOCK OF
RECOGNITION OF
THE   -IN-
THE-   ,
THE   -IN-
THE

HOMI K. BHABHA
"THE WORLD AND THE HOME"

WORLD
HOME
HOME
WORLD

AUTOREN / WRITERS

KOH NGUANG HOW

ist Künstler und Kunstwissenschaftler mit dem Schwerpunkt Singapur. Sein künstlerisches Schaffen seit 1988 umfasst Fotografie, Collage, Assemblage, Installation, Performance, Dokumentation, Archivarbeit, kuratorische Praxis und Forschung.

is an artist and researcher on Singapore art. His artistic practice started in 1988 and encompasses photography, collage, assemblage, installation, performance art, documentation, archiving, curating and research.

MICHAEL LEE

ist Künstler, Kurator und Publizist, wohnhaft in Singapur. Seine Themenfelder sind Urbane Erinnerungen und Fiktionen, besonders im Zusammenhang mit damit verbundenen Verlusten. Er überträgt seine Beobachtungen in Objekte, Diagramme, Installationen ebenso wie in kuratorische Arbeiten und Texte.
http://michaellee.sg

an artist, curator and publisher based in Singapore. He researches urban memory and fiction, especially the contexts and implications of loss. He transforms his observations into objects, diagrams, situations, curations or texts.
http://michaellee.sg

CHARLES MEREWETHER

ist Kunsthistoriker und Publizist zu Kunst aus der Nachkriegszeit und zeitgenössischer Kunst. Er hat an Universitäten in den USA, Mittel- und Südamerika und Australien unterrichtet. Von 1994 bis 2004 war er Kurator der Sammlung des Getty Research Institute in Los Angeles und 2006 künstlerischer Direktor und Kurator der Biennale Sidney. 2007–08 war er stellvertretender Direktor von Cultural District, Saadiyat Island, Abu Dhabi. 2010–2013 war Merewether Direktor vom Institute of Contemporary Arts Singapore.
http://mitpress.mit.edu/authors/charles-merewether

is an art historian and writer on contemporary and postwar art who has taught at universities in the United States, Central and South America, and Australia. Collections Curator at the Getty Research Institute in Los Angeles from 1994 to 2004, he was Artistic Director and Curator for the 2006 Sydney Biennale. Between 2007 and 2008, he was Deputy Director of the Cultural District, Saadiyat Island, Abu Dhabi. From 2010 to 2013, Merewether was Director of the Institute of Contemporary Arts Singapore.
http://mitpress.mit.edu/authors/charles-merewether

ANCA RUJOIU

ist eine rumänische Kuratorin, derzeit in Singapur am NTU CCA – Centre for Contemporary Art und Co-Direktorin von FormContent, einer kuratorischen Intitiative in London. Zuvor koordinierte sie das öffentliche Programm der School of Fine Art am Royal College of Art (UK). Ihr aktuelles Projekt mit FormContent, *It's Moving from I to It* wurde als wanderndes Projekte entwickelt, das als performatives Skript die Abläufe von Produktion und Vertrieb untersucht. Sie war Gastdozentin an verschiedenen Universitäten, darunter u. a. am Goldsmiths College, an der Central Saint Martins University und an der Newcastle University (UK).

is a Romanian curator currently based in Singapore at NTU CCA—Centre for Contemporary Art and co-director of FormContent, a curatorial initiative in London. Previously, she coordinated the public programme of the School of Fine Art at the Royal College of Art (UK). Her recent project with Form Content, *It's Moving from I to It* unfolded as a performative script within a nomadic structure testing formats of production and distribution. She has been a visiting lecturer at various universities including Goldsmiths College, Central Saint Martins University and Newcastle University (UK).

JASON WEE

ist Künstler und Autor. Sein Kunstschaffen befasst sich mit der Aushöhlung der singulären Autorität zugunsten von Polyfonie und Parallaxe. Er transformiert diese singulären Geschichten und Orte in verschiedene visuelle und geschriebene Gegenstände mit besonderer Aufmerksamkeit von Architekturen, Idealismus und unerforschten Zukunftsperspektiven. Wee gründete und führt das Grey Project durch, ein Künstlerraum, Bibliothek und Residenz in Singapur. Er ist ein Redakteur der Lyrikzeitschrift Softblow. Von 2005 bis 2006 war er Atelier Stipendiat im Rahmen des Independent Study Programmes des Whitney Museums. Des Weiteren war Wee u. a. Artist-in-Residence des Artspace in Sydney, des ISEA 2008, des Tokyo Wonder Site sowie des Geyonggi Creation Centeres. Im Jahr 2010 co-organisierte er die Ausstellung *The Future of Exhibition* am Institute of Contemporary Art in Singapur. Die jüngsten kuratorischen Projekte sind die Ausstellungen *Mirrors in the Dark* von Lee Wen (Grey Projects, 2014) und *When You get Closer To The Heart, You May Find Cracks* des Migrant Ecologies Project (NUS Museum, 2014). Wee studierte an The New School und an der Harvard University. Sein zuletzt veröffentlichter Gedichtband mit dem Titel *The Monsters Between Us* wurde von der Zeitung TODAY als eines der besten künstlerischen Werke Singapurs im Jahr 2013 bezeichnet.

is an artist and a writer. His art practice is concerned with the hollowing out of singular authority in favor of polyphony and parallax. He transforms these singular histories and spaces into various visual and written materials, with particular attention to architectures, idealism and unexplored futures. He founded and runs Grey Projects, an artists' space, library and residency in Singapore. He is an editor for Softblow poetry journal. He was a 2005–2006 Studio Fellow at the Whitney Museum Independent Study Program. Artist-in-residencies include Artspace Sydney, ISEA 2008, Tokyo Wonder Site, and Gyeonggi Creation Center. In 2010, he co-organized *The Future of Exhibition* at the Institute of Contemporary Art, Singapore. Recent curatorial projects include *Mirrors in the Dark* by Lee Wen (Grey Projects, 2014) and *When You Get Closer To The Heart, You May Find Cracks* by the Migrant Ecologies Project (NUS Museum, 2014). He studied at The New School and Harvard University. His latest book of poems *The Monsters Between Us,* has been named by TODAY newspaper as one of the top art picks in Singapore of 2013.

MAYEE WONG

ist eine PhD-Anwärterin der Cultural Studies Graduate Group an der University of California, Davis mit einem Schwerpunkt auf ‚Critical Theory'. Gegenwärtig untersucht sie die zeitgenössischen ökologiebezogenen und komplexen systematischen Diskurse der Stadt und von urban design. Ihr Forschungsinteresse umfasst kritische Konzeptionen des Städtischen und des städtischen Raumes, die Geschichte der Technologie, kritische Theorie, Kulturpolitik, visuelle Kultur und Ästhetik sowie militarisierte Logiken und Kultur. Sie ist Mitglied der International Association of Art Critics (AICA) in Singapur.

is a PhD candidate from the Cultural Studies Graduate Group in the University of California, Davis, with a designated emphasis in 'Critical Theory'. Currently examining contemporary ecology-related and complex systemic discourses of the city and urban design, her research interests include critical conceptions of the urban and urban space, history of technology, critical theory, cultural politics, visual culture and aesthetics, and militarised logics and culture. She is also a member of the Singapore chapter of the International Association of Art Critics (AICA).

KÜNSTLER / ARTISTS

ASHLEY YEO (YAKKA)

geb. 1990 in Singapur; 2011–12 Studium der Bildenden Kunst am Chelsea College of Art and Design der University of Arts, London / Masterabschluss mit Auszeichnung; 2007–11 Studium der Bildenden Kunst am LASALLE College of the Arts, Singapur / Bachelor Abschluss (Hons) mit besonderer Auszeichnung; 2014 School of Visual Arts Open Studios, New York / Einzelausstellungen: 2012 *The Lost Children*, Gallery du Monde, London; *Room*, Foxriver Gallery, Singapur; 2011 *A Thousand Words and more*, Orchard Central Kartestudios, Singapur; 2010 *Silent Infatuations*, Trispace, Singapur.

born 1990 in Singapore; 2011–12 MFA (with Merit), Chelsea College of Art and Design, University of Arts, London; 2007–11 BFA (with First Class Honors), LASALLE College of the Arts, Singapore; 2014 School of Visual Arts Open Studios, New York / Solo Exhibitions: 2012 *The Lost Children*, Gallery du Monde, London; *Room*, Foxriver Gallery, Singapore; 2011 *A Thousand Words and more*, Orchard Central Kartestudios, Singapore; 2010 *Silent Infatuations*, Trispace, Singapore.

CHARLES LIM (YI YONG)

schloss sein Studium an der Central Saint Martins School of Art and Design in London mit einem Bachelor in Fine Art ab (2001). Im Folgenden wurde Lim Mitbegründer des bedeutenden Netzkunst Kollektivs tsunamii.net, das an der Documenta11 in Kassel (2002) teilnahm. Er verbindet seine Meereskenntnisse und seine Liebe, Bilder zu machen, indem er begann, sich der Serie *SEA STATE* zu widmen, einer fortlaufenden Arbeit, die bei der Manifesta 7 (2008), der Biennale in Shanghai (2008) und der Singapur Biennale (2011) ausgestellt wurde. Lim's Filme wurden bei dem Internationalen Filmfestival von Rotterdam, dem Tribeca Filmfestival und im Rahmen des Edinburgh Filmfestivals gezeigt. Sein Kurzfilm *All The Lines Flow Out* (2011) hatte seine Premiere beim 68. Filmfestival von Venedig und gewann den Special Mention Award, der erstmals an eine Produktion aus Singapur ging. Das Werk hat seitdem drei weitere Preise bei anderen internationalen Festivals gewonnen. 2015 nimmt er an der 56. Biennale in Venedig teil.

graduated from Central Saint Martins School of Art and Design, London with a B.A. in Fine Art (2001). Lim went on to co-found the seminal net art collective, tsunamii.net, which participated in Documenta11 in Kassel (2002). Combining his knowledge of the sea and his love for making images, he then embarked on the *SEA STATE* series, an ongoing body of work that has been exhibited at Manifesta 7 (2008), the Shanghai Biennale (2008), and at the Singapore Biennale (2011). Lim's moving image works have been screened at the International Film Festival Rotterdam, the Tribeca Film Festival and the Edinburgh Film Festival. His 2011 short film *All The Lines Flow Out* premiered at the 68th Venice Film Festival, winning a Special Mention, the first award ever won there by a Singaporean production. The piece has since received three more awards at other international festivals. He participates in the 56. Venice Biennale 2015.

CHUA CHYE TECK

geb. 1974 in Singapur; 2000 Bachelor of Art, Bildende Kunst – Skulptur, Royal Melbourne Institute of Technology, Campus Singapur; 1996 Diplom, Bildende Kunst – Skulptur, LASALLE-SIA College of the Arts, Singapur; Einzelausstellungen: 2010 *City Landscape*, Künstlerhaus Bethanien, Berlin; 2008 *New Castle*, The Substation, Singapur; *Wonderland*, Wheelock Scotts Square Gallery, Singapur; 2007 *Eternity*, Post-Museum, Singapur; 2001 *Love Story*, The Substation, Singapur; 1996 *It Works Like Magic*, Utopia Gallery, Singapur

1974 born in Singapore; 2000 Bachelor of Arts in Fine Art – Sculpture, Royal Melbourne Institute of Technology, Singapore Campus; 1996 Diploma in Fine Arts – Sculpture, LASALLE-SIA College of the Arts, Singapore; Solo Exhibitions: 2010 *City Landscape (Berlin)*, Künstlerhaus Bethanien, Berlin; 2008 *New Castle*, The Substation, Singapore; *Wonderland*, Wheelock Scotts Square Gallery, Singapore; 2007 *Eternity*, Post-Museum, Singapore; 2001 *Love Story*, The Substation, Singapore; 1996 *It Works Like Magic*, Utopia Gallery, Singapore

hibitions he has taken part in include the 26th Biennale of São Paulo (Brazil, 04), 3rd Fukuoka Asian Art Triennale (Japan, 2005), 1st Singapore Biennale 006), *Thermocline of Art. New Asian Waves* (ZKM, Karlsruhe, Germany, 2007), Country (Guggenheim Museum, New York, 2013). Some of the film festivals at have presented his work include the 41st Director's Fortnight, Cannes International Film Festival (2009), 66th Venice International Film Festival (2009), 65th rlin International Film Festival (2015). He was the subject of profile screenings transmediale 09 (2009) and the 59th Oberhausen Short Film Festival (2013). was recently awarded the grand prize of Asia Pacific Breweries Foundati- Signature Art Prize. He is currently an artist-in-residence at the DAAD, Berlin.

MY SHARMA

b. 1977 in Singapur; 2005–06 Master of Art (Bildende Kunst) am LASALLE College of the Arts, Singapur; 2002–03 Bachelor of Art (Bildende Kunst) mit besonderer Auszeichnung, am Royal Melbourne Institute of Technology (RMIT) University, Melbourne; Einzelausstellungen: 2014 *Factum*, Primae Noctis Gallery, Lugano; *Mode Change*, Michael Janssen Gallery, Singapur; 2013 *Exposition*, Grey Projects, Singapur; 2012 *Apropos*, ICA Gallery 2, Institute of Contemporary Arts, Singapur

77 born in Singapore; 2005–06 Master of Art (Fine Art), LASALLE College of the ts, Singapore; 2002–03 Bachelor of Art (Fine Art) with High Distinction, Royal elbourne Institute of Technology (RMIT) University, Melbourne; Solo Exhibitions: 14 *Factum*, Primae Noctis Gallery, Lugano; *Mode Change*, Michael Janssen Gallery, Singapore; 2013 *Exposition*, Grey Projects, Singapore; 2012 *Apropos*, ICA Gallery 2, Institute of Contemporary Arts, Singapore

Y CHAN

einer der bekanntesten jungen Architekten Singapurs. Er schloss sein Studium an der National University of Singapore mit dem Bachlor of Architecture (1997). Chan gewann den Gold Award bei den 3. SIA Façade Design Excellence Awards 2006 für seine Arbeit am Singapur Pavillon zur Weltausstellung 005 in Aichi, Japan. Er war der hauptverantwortliche Set-and-Stage Designer r nationale und internationale Events: 2005, 2008, 2009, 2011 Singapore National Day Parade; 2008 Singapure Pavillon *Supergarden*, Venedig Biennale

one of Singapore's leading young architects. He graduated from the National University of Singapore with a B.A. of Architecture (1997). Chan won the Gold Award in e 3rd SIA Façade Design Excellence Awards in 2006 for his work on the Singapore vilion at the World Exposition 2005 in Aichi, Japan. He was the principal set-nd-stage designer for both national and international events: 2005, 2008, 2009, 11 Singapore National Day Parade; 2008 Singapor Pavilion *Supergarden*, Venice ennale

PIN PIN

gt mit ihren Filmen den Fokus auf Singapur, ihre Geschichte und ihre Grenzen. e wurden vielerorts in Singapur sowie international in Berlin, Busan, beim Cinéa du Réel, der Viennale, beim Visions du Réel, in Rotterdam, im MOMA und im aherty Seminar sowie im Discovery Channel gezeigt. In Singapur haben die Filme usverkaufte Vorführungen erzielt, wurden in Schulen gezeigt und von Singapore irlines für deren Bordunterhaltungsservice erworben. Pin Pin gewann oder wurde für mehr als 20 Preise nominiert. Der Film *Invisible City* wurde vom Cinéma du éel als „Ein witziges, intellektuell herausforderndes Essay über Geschichte und rinnerung als Mittel zivilen Widerstandes". *Singapore GaGa* wurde von der Straits mes zum besten Film des Jahres 2006 gewählt. Ihr Abschlussfilm *Moving House* t den Student Academy Award für die beste Dokumentation gewonnen. Ihr Film Singapore, with Love über politische Exilanten aus Singapur ist dort verboten. n Pin ist Mitbegründerin von filmcommunitysg, einer Gemeinschaft von unabängigen Filmemachern. Sie war bis vor kurzem Vorstandsmitglied von The Substion, das erste unabhängige zeitgenössische Kunstzentrum in Singapur, und den ational Archives of Singapore.

cuses in her films on Singapore, its histories and its limits. They have screened idely in Singapore and internationally at Berlin, Busan, Cinéma du Réel, Viennale, isions du Réel, Rotterdam, MOMA and at the Flaherty Seminar as well as on

CHUN KAI FENG

geb. 1982 in Singapur; 2010 Masterabschluss Bildende Kunst an der Glasgow School of Art, Glasgow; Einzelausstellungen: 2014 *What Happens When Nothing Happens*, Art Stage: South East Asia Platform 2014, FOST Gallery, Marina Bay Sands Expo Centre, Singapur; 2013 *Nowhere Near*, FOST Gallery, Gillman Barracks, Singapur; 2012 *Stranded*, Hong Kong Art Fair, Chan Hampe Galleries, HKCEC, Hongkong

1982 born in Singapore; 2010 MFA, The Glasgow School of Art, Glasgow; Solo Exhibitions: 2014 *What Happens When Nothing Happens*, Art Stage: South East Asia Platform 2014, FOST Gallery, Marina Bay Sands Expo Centre, Singapore; 2013 *Nowhere Near*, FOST Gallery, Gillman Barracks, Singapore; 2012 *Stranded*, Hong Kong Art Fair, Chan Hampe Galleries, HKCEC, Hong Kong

GERALDINE KANG

geb. 1988 in Singapur, lebt und arbeitet in Singapur; 2007–11 Abschluss mit Auszeichnung als BFA im Studiengang Fotografie und Digitales Bild an der Hochschule für Kunst, Design und Medien der Technischen Universität Nanyang; Einzelausstellung: 2014 *Tell me something I don't know*, Grey Projects, Singapur

1988 born in Singapore, lives and works in Singapore; 2007–11 BFA in Photography And Digital Imaging With Honors (2nd Upper), School of Art, Design and Media, Nanyang Technological University, Singapore; Solo Exhibition: 2014 *Tell me something I don't know*, Grey Projects, Singapore

GRACE TAN

geb. 1979 in Malaysia, lebt und arbeitet in Singapur; 1996–99 Studium Modedesign und -vermarktung am Temasek Polytechnic, Singapur / Diplom mit Auszeichnung; 2009–14 Lehrtätigkeit an der Fakultät für Bildende Kunst der School of the Arts, Singapur; Einzelausstellungen: 2012 *MM*, The Substation Gallery, Singapur; 2008 *kwodrent: working process*, FOST Gallery, Singapur

1979 born in Malaysia, lives and works in Singapore; 1996–99 Diploma (with Merit) in Apparel Design and Merchandising, Temasek Polytechnic, Singapore; 2009–14 Teaching, Faculty of Visual Arts, School of the Arts, Singapore; Solo Exhibitions: 2012 *MM*, The Substation Gallery, Singapore; 2008 *kwodrent: working process*, FOST Gallery, Singapore

HO TZU NYEN

macht Filme, Videoinstallationen und Theaterperformances, die in Verbindung stehen mit seinem Interesse für Philosophie und Geschichte. Seine Arbeiten wurden international in Museen, Galerien sowie im Rahmen von Film- und Kunstfestivals gezeigt. Ho hatte Einzelausstellungen in Singapur (Substation Gallery, 2003; Galerie Michael Janssen, 2013). Er repräsentierte Singapur bei der 54. Biennale in Venedig (2011). Einige Gruppenausstellungen, an denen er beteiligt war, sind die 26. Biennale in São Paulo (Brasilien, 2004), die 3. Fukuoka Asian Art Triennale (Japan, 2005), die 1. Biennale in Singapur (2006) und die Ausstellungen *Thermocline of Art. New Asian Waves* (ZKM, Karlsruhe, Deutschland, 2007) sowie *No Country* (Guggenheim Museum, New York, 2013). Einige der Filmfestivals, die seine Arbeiten gezeigt haben, sind die 41. Director's Fortnight der Internationalen Filmespiele von Cannes (2009), das 66. Internationale Filmfestival Venedig und die 65. Internationalen Filmfestspiele in Berlin. Seine Werke waren ebenso Gegenstand von Aufführungen während der transmediale 09 (2009) und der 59. Internationalen Kurzfilmtage in Oberhausen (2013). Ho Tzu Nyen wurde kürzlich mit dem Großen Preis des Asia Pacific Breweries Foundation Signature Art Prize ausgezeichnet. Zurzeit ist er Artist-in-Residence beim DAAD in Berlin.

makes films, video installations and theatrical performances that are related to his interests in philosophy and history. His works have been shown internationally in museums, galleries, film and performing art festivals. Ho has had one-person exhibitions in Singapore (Substation Gallery, 2003; Galerie Michael Janssen, 2013). He represented Singapore at the 54th Venice Biennale (Italy, 2011). Some group

Discovery Channel. In Singapore, they have received sold out theatrical screenings, toured schools and were acquired by Singapore Airlines for their in-flight entertainment services. Pin Pin has won or been nominated for more than 20 awards. For *Invisible City*, the citation from Cinéma du Réel describes it as "A witty, intellectually challenging essay on history and memory as tools of civil resistance". *Singapore GaGa* was voted the Best Film, 2006 by the Straits Times. *Moving House*, her thesis film won the Student Academy Award for Best Documentary. *To Singapore, with Love*, about Singapore political exiles is banned in Singapore. Pin Pin is a co-founder of filmcommunitysg, a community of independent filmmakers. She was until recently on the Board of The Substation, the first independent contemporary arts centre in Singapore, and the National Archives of Singapore.

VINCE ONG

2008–2009 Studium an der Architectural Association (AA) School of Architecture, London / Abschluss Final (RIBA II) and AA Diplom / 2006–2008 Studium an der Architectural Association (AA) School of Architecture, London / Gruppenausstellungen (Auswahl): 2014 *Sublime Monsters and Virtual Children*", Performance (mit Brian Gothong Tan), Theatre Works 72-13, Singapur / 2010 *Generi-City, Uniquely Singapore, Distinctively London?*, London Design Festival, London / 2007 *You Are Not a Tourist*, Singapore Art Show.

2008–2009 Final Examination (ARB/RIBA Part 2) and AA Diploma, Architectural Association (AA) School of Architecture, London / 2006–2008 Intermediate Examination (ARB/RIBA Part 1), Architectural Association (AA) School of Architecture, London / Group Exhibitions (Selected): 2014 *Sublime Monsters and Virtual Children*, Performance (with Brian Gothong Tan), Theatre Works 72–13, Singapore, 2010 *Generi-City, Uniquely Singapore, Distinctively London?*, London Design Festival, London / 2007 *You Are Not a Touris*", Singapore Art Show

AI TANG

geb. 1984; Einzelausstellungen (Auswahl): 2010 *Sacred Soundscapes*, Esplanade – Theatres on the Bay, Singapur; 2006 *Fuze*, Esplanade – Theatres on the Bay, Singapur

born 1984; Solo Exhibitions (Selected): 2010 *Sacred Soundscapes*, Esplanade – Theatres on the Bay, Singapore; 2006 *Fuze*, Esplanade – Theatres on the Bay, Singapore

IMPRESSUM / IMPRINT

connect: Die Vermessung deiner Wohnung: Singapur unheimlich
connect: The Measure of Your Dwelling: Singapore as Unhomend

ifa-Galerie Berlin
Institut für Auslandsbeziehungen
Linienstraße 139/140
10115 Berlin
17. April bis 05. Juli 2015

ifa-Galerie Stuttgart
Institut für Auslandsbeziehungen
Charlottenplatz 17
70173 Stuttgart
24. Juli bis 04. Oktober 2015

Kurator / Curator
Jason Wee, Singapur

Katalog / Catalogue
Jason Wee, Barbara Barsch, Ev Fischer

Übersetzungen / Translations
Robert Schlicht

Lektorat / Copy-editing
Brian Ring

Redaktionelle Mitarbeit / Editorial assistants
Olivia Braun, Meike Lettau, Eva Spillmann

Gestaltung / Graphic design
Nathanaël Hamon & Florent Moglia
SLANG – Studio for graphic design, Berlin, www.slanginternational.org

Druck / Printing
ruksaldruck, Berlin

Papier
Vorsatz: Sirio Color, perla, 115g/m^2
Inhalt: Symbol Matt Plus, premium white, 150g/m^2, Arcoprint 1 ew, 70g/m^2
von Fedrigoni

Ausstellung / Exhibition
Barbara Barsch, Jason Wee, Ev Fischer, Matthias Merker

Fotonachweis / Photo credits
S./P. 1: Tan Pin Pin, *To Singapore, With Love (In Liebe zu Singapur)*, 2013, video still, 2:01 min
S./P. 20–21: Ho Tzu Nyen, *The Cloud of Unknowing (Die Wolke der Unwissenheit)*, 2011, video still, 28 min
S./P. 152–153: Koh Nguang How
S./P. 160–161, 166–167: Barbara Barsch, *Singapore, February 2014 (Singapur, Februar 2014)*
S./P. 172–173: MayEe Wong

Das Institut für Auslandsbeziehungen e.V. wird gefördert vom Auswärtigen Amt der Bundesrepublik Deutschland, dem Land Baden-Württemberg und der Landeshauptstadt Stuttgart.
The Institute for Foreign Cultural Relations is supported by the German Federal Foreign Office, the state of Baden-Württemberg and the state capital Stuttgart.

www.ifa.de

© 2015 Institut für Auslandsbeziehungen
Text- und Bildautoren / the authors and the artists

ISBN: 978-3-921970-63-8

Mit freundlicher Unterstützung durch / Supported by